THE MOTIVATED MUMMIES' Guide to Confidence

5 Steps to Confidence for You AND Your Child

Tammy Rolfe

THE MOTIVATED MUMMIES' GUIDE TO CONFIDENCE
5 steps to confidence for you AND your child

Copyright ©Tammy Rolfe 2019

ISBN: 978-1-07827-663-4

No part of this publication may be reproduced stored in a retrieval system or transmitted in any form or by any means electronic mechanical photocopying recording scanning or otherwise.

All rights reserved including the right to reproduce this book or portions thereof in any form whatsoever.

The information given in this book should not be treated as a substitute for professional medical advice; always consult a medical practitioner. Any use of information in this book is that of the readers discretion and risk. Neither the author nor the publisher can be held responsible for any loss, claim, or damage arising out of the use, or misuse of the suggestions made, the failure to take medical advice, or for any material on third party websites.

Published by
10-10-10 Publishing
Markham ON

First Publication paperback edition

Contents

Dedication	vii
Foreword	ix
Testimonials	xi
Acknowledgements	xv

Chapter 1: A Life Unlived — 1
My Anxieties Have Anxiety!	1
Cognitive Therapy	4
Stuck!	5
Panic Attacks	8
The Nightmares	9
Protection Bubble	10
Labels Leave Sticky Marks	12
UPW Changed My Life!	14
Importance of Momentum	18
Freedom and Inner Confidence	20
The Birth of the Motivated Mummies	22
Wonder Woman	26

Chapter 2: What Is Confidence? — 31
Step 1: Identify the Problem	31
Confidence Comes with Age	35
Your WHY	37
Action	

Chapter 3: Knowledge Is Power — 41
Step 2: Educate Yourself — 41
Learn and Grow — 45
Learn the Steps — 49
Action — 53

Chapter 4: Be Yourself – Everyone Else Is Taken — 55
Step 3: Accept Who You Are — 55
Whose Eyes Does She Have? — 59
Learn How You Tick — 61
Forgive and Heal — 63
Talk to Yourself Nicely — 66
Action — 67

Chapter 5: Practice What You Preach — 69
Step 4: Take Action — 69
What Does Taking Action Look Like? — 71
Compliment Someone Daily — 72
Eliminate Negative Energy Drainers — 73
The Power of Momentum — 74
Belief Turns to Action — 77

Chapter 6: Food for Thought — 83
Step 5: Be Healthy — 83
Back to Basics — 85
Complex Carbohydrates — 85
Blood Sugar Levels — 86
Protein — 87
Vitamins and Minerals — 89
Good Fats — 89
Food and Drink to Boost Your Brain — 90
Healthy Swaps and Tips — 91
Exercising with Kids — 93
Action — 95
Inspirational Ladies — 97

Chapter 7: It's Magic!	**117**
Bring All Your Joy Faster	117
Visualisation	124
Keeping the Faith	128
Action	129
About the Author	133

> *Jasmine,*
> *Confidence is the most beautiful thing a woman can wear!*

I dedicate this book to my loving, supportive family, who are always there for me, and to all the motivated mums working hard to build a happier life for their family.

Foreword

Would you like to build your confidence in any area of your life? *The Motivated Mummies Guide to Confidence* by Tammy Rolfe is designed for you to gain quick and easily actionable ways to do just that. Not only can you use the book to accelerate your own confidence, but Tammy has designed it to be simple so you can use it to help your child as well. Her action points throughout the book help you to stay on track, and adjust the plan to meet your own individual needs. You decide what you need and what is achievable for you and your family, and Tammy will help you reach your goal.

When I met Tammy in November 2018, I was amazed by her story. It was hard to believe she ever suffered from anxiety and social phobia as she stood so proudly on the stage. Her charisma and personality shone through as she spoke of her business of transforming mothers and creating happier family lives. I particularly liked how she teaches a good work life balance for mums, as this is something I feel is particularly important.

It is obvious to me that Tammy has the ability to connect with you on a deep level, and has the skills and knowledge to help you move to your desired outcome. She can be a great mentor and coach to you, helping you to achieve more from your life. I love her motto: BE THE PERSON YOU WANT YOUR CHILD TO BE.

Read Tammy's book to gain the strength she has provided within the pages, and the guidance you need to take the action to make the changes you want to see in your life.

Raymond Aaron
New York Times Bestselling Author

Testimonials

"Tammy Rolfe is a friend of mine. I was honoured to share the stage with her, and I suggest you work with her, because I'm going to."

James MacNeil
Author, international speaker, coach & founder of
Pure Spiritual Intelligence

"Tammy's workshops at our events have been a great success. Feedback from participants has been very positive. One gentleman even said that she had completely changed his perspective."

Linda Tabor-Thomas
Co-founder of Slough Happiness Collective

"Tammy Rolfe *is* transformation, like a dry, Savannah brush fire. Give her one spark of inspiration, and she lights herself on fire with it and runs through the world, igniting everyone in her path!"

Raphael Paquin
Transformational personal and business coach
Life Growth Designs

"I love Tammy's workshop, as it makes me push myself, and with the information and support she gives, it gives me the tools to make real changes needed to improve my life."

Charlene
Befriending co-ordinator at Mind (a charity for better mental health)

"After being a client of Tammy's for over a year, I can honestly say that she helps you see impossible dreams as possible. She gives you ambitious but practical guidance to overcome hurdles or self- doubt. I highly recommend Tammy for anyone looking for a breakthrough in life."

"Tammy has a unique talent for helping you get back on track when you've lost your way and are full of self-doubt. She knows instinctively how to guide you through the maze and get you back on track to the life you want. Tammy has plenty of life experience to draw on, as well as her formal training. If you need to stop spinning in circles, and start getting what you want from life, Tammy can drive you there."

"Oh, my goodness, one hour with Tammy has given me so much value and loads to think about! Her energy and passion is contagious! I would highly recommend her as someone to work with. She is very knowledgeable and experienced. Her own story is 100% inspirational, and the way she has turned her life around is incredible. I have no doubt she would be able to help any mum in business who is struggling with anxiety, confidence, and getting the balance right in their life. Thank you, Tammy, I have taken so much away from our call today, which will definitely improve my life."

"Tammy is such an authentic, honest, and real person, and a natural coach. She isn't afraid of challenge, and lives by her teachings on her own personal growth journey. This is what makes her so relatable and likeable and gets her clients results. Tammy has helped me to break through something I have always struggled with. I hate exercise but

Testimonials

always feel that I should be doing it for my health, but I never do, so then I feel bad about it. Tammy helped me to realise that I'm not going to do it, because I don't want to. So, I now incorporate exercise into everyday life, by jogging back from nursery drop off, playing tag with the kids, and running with them on their bikes. It hasn't taken up any time, I am a better mum, and I have more fun! Thank you, Tammy!"

"I had a one-hour mindset session with Tammy, and WOW, I feel so much better. She really helped me focus and change my mindset pattern for the better. I would recommend Tammy to anyone looking for coaching or help with anxiety."

Acknowledgements

I would like to take this opportunity to thank the special people in my life, and those who have helped me along on my journey. Your part, however big or small, has got me to where I am today, and for that, I am extremely grateful.

Mum, my rock
Thank you for your continued love and support in everything I do. You are forever there for me, and I know that you always have my back. It is your natural coaching skills and strength of character that has enabled me to not only help myself but to help many others too. You are the strongest, most determined woman I have ever met, and I am proud to be your daughter.

Steve, my best friend
We met when I was not in a good place, but you loved me anyway. You care for me and make me laugh on a daily basis. I have grown so much in the last 7 years, and you have given me the space and freedom to do so. Your support and encouragement mean the world to me, and I am so very proud to now be called your wife. Thank you for being a great role model to the girls, and for caring for them like you do.

Olivia, my beautiful angel
My firstborn, you are like an angel because you were always so well behaved and easy to care for, and people often commented on how good you were. You are so special. For so many years, you kept me going without even realising it. You were given responsibilities well

beyond your years, and you excelled throughout. I am so proud of you. Always follow your dreams, and never give up.

Heidi, my beautiful little one
You will always be my little Heidi Ho, so special and unique. You didn't have it easy as a baby, but you have certainly pulled yourself up and turned into one amazing young lady! I am so proud of you and your attitude toward life. You make me want to be a better person just to keep up with you! I look forward to watching your incredible future unfold, and I trust that you will create it perfectly.

My family
We may not always see eye to eye, but we are always there for each other. I thank you for every treasured memory, every giggle and every fight, every tale being told, and the precious times that we have been so close. No family is perfect, but you are all perfectly mine. You have helped shape me into who I am today, and I will always love you.

My friends
Bonita, Billy, Sue, Wendy, Paula, Joelle, Caroline, Jenny, Becki, Louise, Felicity, Chelle, Christine, Kimberly, Pina, Michelle, Lindsay, Sinead, Sharon, Fiona, Kelly, Kim, Sandra, Charles, Ernestine, Shawnee, Syane, and Linda, to name but a few....

You have all been there at one time or another to pick me up and help me carry on. You have been a shoulder to cry on or a friendly face to laugh with, and always there if I needed you. You have never made demands or criticized; you have taken me for who I am, and supported me on my journey, for good and bad. I am always here for you, just as you have been there for me. Love you lots.

My Inspirational Ladies
Nayan Mistry, Lisa Huse, Bridget Du Haime, Heather Humphries, Samantha Francis, Louvaine Hunt, Mairi Holden, Marayam Akram and Khateeba Chechi, thank you so much for sharing your stories and helping to inspire and motivate other mothers.

Acknowledgements

Dr Gareth Ward
My chiropractor: Thank you for fixing my body from the tight and twisted mess it was, and for helping to calm my nervous system after years of abuse. You started me off on my journey by introducing me to Tony Robbins, and although I know you knew he would help me, I'm sure you had no idea to what extreme! I will always be very grateful to you.

Nimi Padda
At the risk of sounding completely nuts, you shared the law of attraction with me, and I have benefited from it ever since. Because of you, I have taught many people the secret, and I have helped changed so many lives, including my children, and for that, I am forever grateful. Keep on sharing the love.

James MacNeil
Author, international speaker, and trainer of all that is wise! I was so grateful to meet you and be able to spend 5 great days in your company, and I learnt so much. You say you always like to give more than you promise, and you certainly do. I look forward to sharing the stage with you one day.

Raymond Aaron
New York Times bestselling author, top speaker and expert in communication, and my publisher! I have enjoyed your teachings immensely, and I am extremely grateful for the help and support you have given me, to enable me to get my message out there. You have made the process of writing my book so achievable that there is absolutely no reason everyone can't have their story out in the world. Having mild dyslexia and not being the most academic girl, you and your team filled me with confidence and had faith that I could write just as well as the next person. Thank you and thank you for wanting to publish my book.

Toastmasters Windsor Speakers
A big thank you to all the supportive attendees at my Toastmasters group, especially Christine, Gulbin, Kam, Robert, Tony, Jocelyn and Leela, for making me feel so welcome.

My Coaches

Raphael Paquin
Life Growth Designs

Laura Kingston
Leap Career Coaching

Catalina Park
Mindset Coach

Thomas Leverington
Personal Trainer

Rob Du Haime
Health & Life Coach

Chris Leslie
Life Coach for the Real You

Bridgett Tulloh
Life Coach

Brody Lee
Energy & Business Coach

Over the last 2 years, each of you has played a part in my transformation. Whether it has been a big part (Raphael) or a slightly smaller role, you have encouraged, supported, and guided me to be the strong and confident person I am today. We all have our weak

Acknowledgements

points, and we all have the odd limiting belief pop up here and there. This, as we know, is perfectly normal, and it is the reason why everyone needs a coach! Life is a rollercoaster, especially if you are aiming high and striving to meet life goals. I have learnt so much, but I will always benefit from having one-on-one support.

Each time I reach the top, I will need that gentle (or not so gentle, with some of you) encouragement to go out of my comfort zone and keep on striving forward. I don't do this because I am unhappy with what I have, I, like you, know there is a big, wide world out there, full of possibilities, and I see no reason why I shouldn't grab it all with both hands while I am here to do so! I lived a life so unfulfilled and so scared for so long that I refuse to live like that anymore, so thank you all from the bottom of my heart.

And of course….
Tony Robbins
Author, philanthropist, life coach, and so much more!
Without your courage, strength, and determination to succeed, my life would never have been transformed the way it was. You say things in a way that no one else has ever said them, and you have taken massive, brave, determined action in the past to be the hugely successful person you are today, changing millions of lives. I literally owe my life to you and can never thank you enough. You give me the determination to pursue my dreams in the aim of changing thousands of lives for the better. I have taken, and will continue to take, massive action, as one day I may save a life like you have. Many heartfelt thanks, from me as well as all those I am now helping to live happier lives.

Chapter 1

A Life Unlived

My Anxieties Have Anxiety!

If you have picked this book up but are wondering if it is really that important to fix this problem of low confidence, or if your child is making up how bad they are feeling, then I would like to start by giving you an insight into the life of an anxious, unconfident person. I understand that everyone is different, and my anxiety could be worse or better than yours or your child's, but a glimpse into an unconfident life will hopefully help motivate you to work through the book and tackle any issues that you are facing right now.

It's hard to remember exactly what my anxiety was like, now that it has gone. I know it was crippling, but it was also so natural to feel that way—it just felt like me. I would worry about absolutely everything! This included the way I looked, and even the way others looked. I had zero confidence. I remember sitting in a restaurant once, and there was a family of four sitting across from us. The dad was eating, and he had food on his face, but no one at his table made any reference to this (probably as they were all eating, and it did not bother anyone). For me, this was torture, and I didn't even know the man! It put my stomach in knots just because I knew how I would feel if it had been myself with food on my face. I could not help looking at him, worried about how he would feel when he found out about it. I was constantly wiping my own face, with the paranoia that I too had food on my face! If you can understand what I felt, then I deeply feel for you. To worry about yourself is exhausting, but to worry about the whole world is just debilitating.

You do not realise, when you're going through it, just what a struggle it is to live with low self-esteem and anxiety. When you have had it for so long, it's just a way of life, and you forget what it feels like to feel calm, relaxed, and confident. Slowly, you adapt to the situations that you are in, and people around you adapt to you too. I remember, when I was about 16, I was at a family buffet, and I attempted to get the food myself, but the combination of holding the plate, standing at a table with other people, and leaning across the food, picking it up, was too much. My shaky hands were obvious for everyone to see, and the stress of getting the food from one plate to another without dropping it literally made my stomach turn. I think you can only fully understand this feeling if you have been through it yourself, because to an outside person, it sounds crazy. I was standing next to the people that loved me the most, and people that were the least likely to judge me, in an environment where I'm meant to be calm and happy, yet I was worried over dropping a little bit of food onto the table. I was not confident enough to serve myself food! My low self-esteem and lack of confidence caused my anxiety, and it was not rational, and it does not make sense, but that is what anxiety is like—it's not rational. As time went on, I avoided these situations, and sometimes I would avoid going to events completely. Other times, I would just ask my family to go and get me some food. Right or wrong, they did it because they loved me, and they did not want to see me suffering when I didn't have to.

I don't remember there ever being a time when I had confidence. I must have had it at some point, as we are not born with low self-esteem. Looking back at old photos, I had lots of experiences and fun times. I even used to go up on stage when we went away on our holidays to the caravan parks. I was entered into all sorts of competitions, beauty contests, fancy dress-ups, and games—I was up for anything, so I suppose that takes confidence. I just didn't realise it at the time. It was normal. My mum and dad made that normal for me.

I had no thoughts when I was young as to what I looked like. I was me, and that was that. It wasn't until I started school that the negative connotations regarding my looks crept in—children can be so cruel. I was probably average looking, but I was hairy—really hairy! I was light skinned and had dark brown hair on my arms, legs, and upper lip… oh, and on my nose; don't forget the nose! I wasn't so bothered about my legs, because most people had hairy legs, but my face really got to me. I was called "hairy," "man," and "gorilla," on a regular basis. Life was different in those days; people didn't go to salons as much as they do now, and it was definitely not common to take your 8-year-old to get a wax. My mum sympathised with my situation, I'm sure, but I don't recall her doing anything about it. Maybe she didn't know how much it affected me; but maybe she tried?

At 8 years old, it did not cross my mind to take matters into my own hands (I wonder if that is why I am such a control freak now?), so I just suffered with the bullying. I remember feeling very ugly during my school days. I had friends—lots of friends—so I felt loved and liked, but ugly. Each comment about my hairy body was like a knife to my chest, which got pushed deeper and deeper. It did not help my situation to have an exceptionally pretty sister—she came 3rd in the beauty pageant at school. So, not only was I being told on a regular basis that I looked like a gorilla, I was also being told how pretty my sister was. Grown adults would say, in front of me, "Oh, she's so pretty." How rude! Yes, she was, and still is, very pretty, but don't say it in front of me. That's not going to help my confidence issue. They probably didn't think of how it would affect me, and they were just stating the obvious. They also didn't know that I had an imagined problem going on.

At 11, I was allowed to shave my legs, and my mum finally took me to get my top lip waxed, to get ready for secondary school, but the damage had been done. I had received too many comments for too long, and on top of that, my dad had just left our family. So, I not only felt ugly, I felt extremely unloved now too. He also took my best friend with him when he left, so I didn't even have my friend to have my back in my new, scary, secondary school. Doesn't life just kick you in the teeth sometimes? I have many reasons for losing my confidence, and maybe one reason was enough, or maybe it was a combination of them all, but they are reasons, not excuses. It took me 20 years to work out that I did not have to hold on to these old stories. They happened, and they were true, but to keep holding on to them was no benefit at all.

If you have a lack of confidence, or your child has a lack of confidence, it has come from somewhere. Maybe it was not as dramatic as my story, or maybe it was worse, but you were not born with low self-esteem—it was created. But the good news is, if low self-esteem was created, confidence can be created too! You just need to reverse the process and let go of what does not benefit you.

Cognitive Therapy

When I was 17, I went for cognitive therapy. This is when negative thought patterns about yourself, or about the world, are challenged in order to alter unwanted behaviour. This is known to help anxiety and depression, and it was extremely useful, and it did, after many sessions, allow me to participate in more activities than I had done before. The idea behind my cognitive therapy was to continuously put me in situations that I would normally avoid, and mark myself out of 10 to gage how uncomfortable I felt: 1 being not bad at all; 6 being a shaky mess; and 10 being full on panic attacks or complete avoidance. The concept of the therapy was very good, and it did help with some of the negative talk going on in my head, but if only I had been able to add in some of the techniques I have recently learnt, the therapy would have been a huge success, and I would not have wasted years being unhappy. As it was, I continued to put myself in these situations, and I learnt to live with the anxiety, not because I was cured but just because I got more used to the feelings. I got used to living an uncomfortable life and started to forget what feeling good felt like. I am grateful that the doctors didn't just put me straight onto antidepressants at a young age, and that they did try to go down the therapy route first. Sadly, the antidepressants came later.

"Try to understand the blackness, lethargy, hopelessness, and loneliness they're going through. Be there for them when they come through the other side. It's hard to be a friend to someone who's depressed, but it is one of the kindest, noblest, and best things you will ever do."
– Stephen Fry

Stuck!

Have you ever felt completely stuck—you can't go forward, and you can't go back? That's how I felt when I was young. I was stuck, in more ways than one. I desperately wanted to go back to how my family had been—a daddy's girl, with lots of fun and laughter—but that was not possible. Yet I did not know how to move forward either; I did not know how this new life worked. I couldn't navigate my way around it, and I had no knowledge or skills to get me through.

I wanted to move on from my lack of confidence and low self-esteem, but it felt impossible. I had numerous councillors telling me that I was like this because my dad left, and that I was feeling abandoned and unloved by him. Well, how was that ever going to change? Surely, that meant I was always going to feel like this—stuck—because he's never coming back. Then, there's the biggy: life. I was scared on a daily basis—scared to go out, scared to look in the mirror, scared of how awful I felt, scared to live. Then, on the flip side of that, I was scared to die. I was absolutely terrified of dying. I had a huge fear of death for most of my life, and I now know this is very common for people who suffer from anxiety. We need to be in control of everything, and the one thing we can't control is death, and that scares the life out of us. I know I am not alone in having thought about ending my life, and I believe it is a lot more common than people think. Why wouldn't you, when you are going through something so painful, and you cannot see an end in sight?

It is a strange concept to get your head around—fearing death so much, yet thinking of ending your life so often—but it wasn't so much that I wanted to die as I wanted the pain to stop, and I could see no other way out of it. If you are feeling this way now, I beg you to seek help, and you might have to try numerous people or groups until you get the help you need, but there IS a way out, and life really can be amazing. Whatever you have been through or are going through, there is always hope, and always a way forward.

www.samaritans.org: You can call the Samaritans any time, day or night, for whatever you're going through, from any phone, for FREE. Call 116 123, or write them an email, as sometimes writing down your thoughts and feelings can help you understand them better.

jo@samaritans.org: Response time: 24 hours
Mind info 0300 123 3393 or text 86463

I now realise the vast waste it would have been if I had done anything irrational, and I am forever grateful for the love and support I had from my family on a daily basis. It was their love that kept me going, as I could not hurt them in that way, and I knew they wanted me around. Death is a funny topic; it is rarely spoken of, and yet it affects every single person on the planet. We will all die one day, so why don't we speak of it? Is it just too scary to conceive?

Having had such a fear, I make a concerted effort to talk about it with my immediate family. It gives me comfort to know how they feel about death (My daughters are surprisingly okay with it, with the younger one describing it as an adventure!), and what they will do after I pass. I tell them to not be sad for me, and to do the best they can in life, as we are only here once (or are we?). I tell them to scatter my ashes, so they are not restricted to visiting me or keeping a grave neat and tidy. I do not want to be a burden on them. We joke often about my bench that I would like, and we come up with weird and wacky places for it to be placed. They often joke that a scruffy log in a dirty park would be fine, or that I could share someone else's bench, and they'll scratch my name on it too. I love this, as when I am gone, I know they will laugh when they see benches with names on them, as it will remind them of our conversations.

We cannot eliminate all our fears. I am still scared of dying, but for a different reason now—I'm really enjoying my life! We can ease our own pain of fears by changing our thinking around the subject, talking to others so we are not guessing the answers, and putting action plans in place to help us feel more in control. So, as I write this, I have just found this quote for you:

> "People living deeply have no fear of death."
> – Anais Nin

And I have to be honest, it has made me think… Am I still scared of dying because I haven't fulfilled my mission yet? Am I still holding back from giving everything I have to offer; is this why I am afraid to die? Maybe… What would you like to achieve during your time on this earth?

> "Whatever you want to do, do it now.
> There are only so many tomorrows."
> – Michael Landon

Panic Attacks

Panic attacks are caused by fear—usually fear of death or pain. My panic attacks were most often whilst I was driving my children in the car. My mum's going to have a heart attack if she ever reads this. I didn't realise they were panic attacks to start with, but my heart would race, and I would become hot and have waves of sleep come over me. The waves were so bad that I literally felt like I was going to fall asleep at the wheel. This happened many times and, at first, I thought it was because I was tired, so I made sure I only drove when I was well rested and not after a big meal that can make you sleepy. It was not until much later that I realised it was anxiety; and thankfully, I now have the strategies I need to counteract the feelings if they pop up. They have done so, occasionally, whilst driving fast on the motorway. A negative thought will pop into my head, making my thought train charge off down the "oh, my goodness, we're going to die" track. Before, in the old days, I wasn't even aware I was thinking such negative thoughts. They were all so natural to me, they would sit consistently in the background. Now I can spot them quickly and take action before they get hold.

I was a single mum for 8 years, so I often took my girls away by myself, meaning I was the one that had to drive. It was a standing joke on our trips that I was well stocked up with wine gum sweets. I'm not sure if the girls thought I was just greedy on our travels, but I ate them to help me think about something other than crashing, and I honestly thought, at the time, I needed the sugar to keep me awake. I now know they helped me to change my focus, and I had started developing my attack strategy that I will explain later in the book.

If someone had told me that just two years later I would be receiving messages from teenagers and adults, thanking me for helping them out of their panic attacks and relaying stories of new ventures they were having because of my help, I never would have believed them. It gives me an even greater buzz to improve other people's lives than it does my own! I feel honoured and blessed that they have trusted me, and I also thank the Universe for giving me the experiences of my previous panic attacks so I can help my clients progress quicker. Having the understanding of how they are feeling helps me to meet them where they are, and walk with them to a calmer, happier place. Stopping panic attacks is all about breaking the cycle of negative thought patterns. You may not even realise you have a negative thought pattern to start with, and this may need to be pointed out to you (This is why I prefer coaching over counselling, as coaches are allowed to point things out if appropriate.), which can speed up your results. Once you identify the negative thought, you can work on adapting it until it is no longer your predominate thought. Please never label a child as having anxiety if they have panic attacks; say that it's something they are experiencing, and they will find a way past it. This goes for yourself too. Panic attacks are caused by a thought; change the thought and you change the effect on your body. Once a child is labelled, it is much harder to break.

*"If you do what you've always done,
you'll get what you've always gotten."*
– Tony Robbins

The Nightmares

I suffered with nightmares most nights. It didn't matter what I watched on telly the night before, if I ate cheese or didn't eat cheese, or if I thought happy things before I went to bed. Every night, I would have a dream that made me feel uncomfortable or scared. I would wake up exhausted, like I'd lived through a traumatic event, night after night. They were so real that sometimes I would not be able to untangle the dream from reality. I would wake up tired even though I had a solid 8 hours sleep, and I carried the nightmare around for the rest of the day. Those feelings that I felt, they were so real that I kept them with me, hovering over my head like a black cloud. Sometimes I couldn't recall my dreams, but I could recall the feeling of them, and these were the worst dreams. The anxiety that they caused, and the discomfort in my body, was just awful. I always tried to remember my dreams as soon as I woke up, because I found going over them again would at least explain the feelings later in the day. I don't remember when the nightmares started, but I do recall when they ended. They literally stopped when my anxiety stopped. It was like a tap being turned off. No more nightmares—lots of dreams but no nightmares—and no waking up with that sinking horrible feeling. I don't miss those at all.

ACTION

There are things you can do if you or your child suffers with nightmares. Obviously, if you have generalised anxiety, like I did, you need to address that, but if not, you can follow these tips:

- Relax before bed; take time to destress and wind down.
- Do not go on social media straight before bed. It can cause negative thoughts without you realising it.
- Read or watch an upbeat book or program.
- Once in bed, think back through your day, and try and find your best bit. This will help you to pull out all your good memories of the day to find the best one.
- Be prepared for anything happening the next day so you are not worrying in advance.
- Ensure your environment is comfortable and safe.

> *"I believe in hard work, but I believe in vindication as well. You have a few nightmares, I imagine, before you reach your dream."*
> –Cody Rhodes

Protection Bubble

The specialists said that my anxiety and depression started after my dad left when I was nearly 11, but I can recall being crouched down in my living room at the age of maybe four or five, next to the sofa, crying over a song. I think that sometimes we get mixed up between being sensitive and being depressed. Being sensitive means you are open to feelings more, and you take on everybody else's feelings and emotions. Of course, there are thousands of people around us, so someone is bound to be sad or troubled, and as sensitive people, we soak that up like a sponge. Maybe we just need to learn how to put a barrier up to protect ourselves a little bit, so we can still empathize, but we just don't take it in as much.

I learnt I needed to protect myself during my time as a beautician. Most beauticians and therapists are of a caring nature, and most I know are very sensitive to the emotions and actions of others. It is part of the job to allow your patient to offload their problems during their time with you. It doesn't matter what treatment they are having; they talk about their woes, and they go out feeling a lot lighter than when they came in. They know that their problems will not go any further, and just to talk about it helps to reduce the burden. When I first started out as a beautician, I used to take these problems and carry them on my shoulders, each client piling more and more onto me. I felt responsible to help them, and saddened when I couldn't. During my journey of self-help, I read teachings of Burt Goldman, The American Monk. He helped me to learn how to have empathy for others without absorbing their emotional baggage. This has been an important skill in my life and career, and I feel it has helped me a huge amount. You must do whatever it takes to protect yourself and keep yourself strong. If you are not in a good, happy place, you are not able to help others to the best of your ability. It does not benefit you, or them, to take on their emotions and feelings, and it is 100% possible to be the same kind and caring person without letting their negative energy in.

"Do not give in too much to feelings. An overly sensitive heart is an unhappy possession on this shaky earth."
– Johann Wolfgang von Goethe

ACTION

Look Burt Goldman up for his full advice, but basically, he taught me to touch the roof of my mouth with my tongue, and as I did this, I was to imagine a cascade of armour dropping from the top of my head! I imagined it like slats of armour, each dropping one at a time to form a protective barrier. It is this physical action combined with the mental picture that helps you to avoid taking in unwanted energy. Have a look around, and you may find a technique you like better. Some use radiating light from their own bodies; others use a mirror—there are many ways, so you can find what suits you. Teaching this technique to a sensitive child is a great idea and could give them comfort in difficult situations.

Labels Leave Sticky Marks

I don't recall exactly when my label got stuck on me, but I was always very aware that I was the depressed one. There were 5 children in my family as I was growing up, and in my eyes, we all had a label… I was *the depressed one*. My eldest sister was *the black sheep* (pretty sure she gave herself this label as I never heard anyone else call her this), and my second eldest sister was *the golden child*, although on later reflection, both her and my parents didn't know about this, so was that just my reality of it? My eldest brother was *the incredible sulk*, since he was in his room alone a lot (pretty sure dad started that one off), and then my younger brother… I'm not sure what his label was—maybe *the baby* to start with, and then *the naughty one*—but I'm sure he had one.

Our parents didn't hand out these labels as we were born, like birth certificates. We must have just picked them up along the way. That's the danger of labels: They are very easy to attach, and once you have one, it is very hard to get rid of, and there is always a bit of sticky left attached somewhere. Once you have received this label, by yourself or someone else, not only have you got to get over your issue, but if you do get over it, you lose your personality, because if you're not that person, (insert label) then who the hell are you, and where do you fit in your family? This is why some people find it so hard to change an unwanted habit, because it is so tightly built into their identity. The fear of losing their identity is way bigger than the current situation.

Imagine yourself as an odd-shaped puzzle piece—odd-shaped with all your imperfections—but as odd as you are, you still fit into that puzzle board. Now, imagine smoothing out some of those edges, getting the help you need to overcome your issues. Now you're not so odd-shaped anymore, and you're not so imperfect anymore; in fact, you like yourself, but you're now a round peg. You don't fit in your misshapen family puzzle board. So where do you fit? How can you belong in your family when you have lost your place on the board? You lose the feeling of being connected with your loved ones. This is the problem with having a label.

So, what is the answer? Talk about it. Talk to your family, and ask them who they see you as, and how they feel about you now that you have changed. I'm quite confident they wouldn't reply the way you think they would. Quite often, we feel we have changed huge amounts, and it will be a big shift for the whole family, but in reality, each family member is concentrating on themselves, and your reality is not their reality. They may not even see your dramatic change as dramatic. They may see that you smile more now, or you are more confident now, or you are just happier. Unstick your label and let it go; let yourself be moulded into the person that you truly want to be, and you will find that you do still fit in your family board, and there will always be a space for you.

"There's nothing that makes you more insane than family. Or more happy. Or more exasperated. Or more... secure."
– Jim Butcher

UPW Changed My Life!

In April 2017, my life took a dramatic turn. I was feeling particularly down, to the point where I was wandering around the streets at midnight, trying to decide whether to stick around. On paper, I had it all: two beautiful daughters; a loving partner; a great home; my own business, which I loved; and a supportive family. What more could I possibly want? That's what most people kept saying to me:

"What more do you want? You are never happy. You've got everything you asked for. When will you ever be satisfied?"

I did have everything I asked for, because I made a point of getting it. I strongly believed in the law of attraction. I believed, and still do believe, that if you ask for something, you can get it.

I had lived like that for 5 years, and I had received my beautiful home, my loving partner, my amazing children, and my successful business. What I hadn't achieved was my good mental health. I hadn't achieved a feeling of comfort in my own skin. I had an underlying sense of unhappiness, and my whole life was filled with anxiety. Even though I had it all, in my eyes, I had nothing, because I was so desperately unhappy with myself. Happiness begins from within. If you are not happy with yourself, then you can't fix everything around you to make yourself happy. It just doesn't work like that. One night was particularly bad, and I was walking around the streets where I live, close to midnight, just trying to decide what I wanted to do with my life. I'm ashamed to admit it, but I was tempted to not even bother carrying on with it. Things had really hit rock bottom.

It would have been hard for anybody to realise from the outside, because from their eyes, I had probably hit rock bottom many years before. My house had been close to being repossessed, I struggled to put food on the table, I was borrowing money off my mum just to feed the kids and clothe them, and I was paying solicitors fees, using up all my savings. That was rock bottom, from the outside world. For me, this was not rock bottom, because I still had hope that when things got better, I would be happy. But now... if I had it all and I still wasn't happy, where the hell do I go from there? A couple of days later, my chiropractor, Dr Gareth, suggested I look up a man called Tony Robbins, and he sent me a link, for which I will be forever grateful. I clicked on the link, and it had an article about the six human needs—I didn't understand a word of it. But when you're on the internet, one link leads to another, which leads to something else, and I finally came to a post on an article about UPW (Unleash the Power Within), a 4-day seminar in London.

At the time, I was still suffering from social phobia, anxiety, and depression, and I very rarely went out anywhere without Steve, my children, or my mum, because I just didn't feel okay by myself. The thought of going was terrifying, and although I had money now, I didn't have a spare £800 for the ticket plus the cost of the hotel. There were lots of other reasons I shouldn't have gone. My eldest daughter had two important school things going on, and I had the guilt of leaving the little one on the Easter holidays, so I really should have stayed at home. I mean, who was going to look after everyone, and run the house, walk the dogs, get the shopping, etc. Mums are always in demand one way or another, yet a week earlier, I was ready to kill myself, as I felt no one needed me. This alone proves that our minds talk bollox, and sometimes we need to just realise that.

Something inside me told me this was right, and I just felt such a huge pull to go to this event that I borrowed the money from good old bank of mum, and I signed up for my hotel and ticket! Literally, 4 weeks later, my partner was driving me to the London Excel for the 4-day event. I was terrified as usual. Usually, my hands would shake, but this time my whole body was shaking, and I felt sick. Even though I had signed up, and I was there ready to participate, I did not have any faith that these 4 days would solve my problems. How could they, when so many had tried before? I remember getting out of the car, giving Steve a kiss, and saying, "I don't know if I'm coming back." He laughed and gave me a kiss back, and said, "I'll pick you up on Sunday." Even he did not know how bad I was feeling inside. You hear of women just running away, and you always wonder what could possibly be going through their minds for them to leave their families. Well, I'll tell you what was going through my mind: I didn't feel needed; I didn't feel particularly wanted; I didn't feel important; and I honestly didn't think that I would be that missed if I did go. The biggest reason that I would have walked away and never went back was a belief that if I just ran away, far enough away, then I would eventually lose the problems. I hear this a lot in my coaching sessions. My clients dream of moving away—some to new homes; some to new areas of the country—and each situation is the same. They believe that if they have a different setting, their life will be different. If they can just change the environment they are in, then everything will be okay. The trouble with that is that the problems are in your head, and it doesn't matter how far you run, or where you run to, those problems will stay with you.

I am so grateful that I was drawn to that event in April 2017, because it was truly 100% life changing. I walked in to register in the vast registration hall, and there were thousands of people queuing for this event. As I held my shaky hand out to have my wristband attached to me, the lady asked me if I was okay. I told her that I felt quite sick with nerves. She smiled and said, "I'm sure you'll be fine, but there's a medical room down the hall if you need it." I carried on to where I was supposed to be sitting, and looked around. I could not believe it. I was sitting in a room with 10000 other people. Ten thousand! For me, a crowd was 3 or 4 people, so to be sitting around all these people, without any of my support systems (my favourite people) around me, I really was terrified.

I would need a much bigger book to explain what Tony Robbins did for me over the 4 days, but let me just say that when I walked into that event, I was at rock bottom; and when I came out, I was flying so high that 2 years later, I still haven't come back down. One of the first tasks he got us to do was to turn to our neighbour, look them in the eye, and say, "I own you." I had always struggled to look people in the eye, but I didn't even feel worthy of owning the chair that I was sitting on, let alone the person that was standing next to me. I couldn't say it. Four days later, 1 fire walk, and a million high fives, and I owned every f***** in that room, and I wasn't afraid to tell them! Tony Robbins had achieved what no therapist over the last 20 years had even touched on. He enabled me to let go of the burdens that I was carrying, and to dig deep and find the inner confidence and self-belief that I had been missing for so long. I remember, every evening after the event, or during the break, I would quickly rush out to phone my mum, and I would scream to her, "I can't believe it; I feel amazing! I just can't even imagine what we will be doing tomorrow that would make me feel better than today. I'm so happy!" Then, the next day, he would do something even more incredible, and I would be on the phone even more hysterical to Mum, sometimes with tears rolling down my face, just at the amazement of how different I felt. So, if you are thinking about getting help, or you feel a pull to something that could benefit your life, just go and do it. It doesn't matter about the material things you have around you—if you don't have your inner happiness, you really don't have anything.

I had been a beautician for 10 years and absolutely loved my job. I love to help people, but after attending the UPW, I felt I had found my true meaning. You hear people say they have a calling, but I don't think you truly understand until you have one yourself. I have seen so many therapists and counsellors, but having learnt the strategies that Tony teaches, I was 100% sure that this was what I wanted to do with the rest of my life. I wanted to teach other people how they too could break free of such misery and pain, and live a life of freedom, like I had just learnt to do.

Importance of Momentum

Most people, when they get advice, hear it, but they don't take action. There is only a small percentage of people who are so teachable and so motivated and driven that they literally put everything they hear into action. You are one of those motivated people. You would not be reading this book if you weren't. It is people like you that will succeed greatly in life. I came back from UPW, after having been there for 4 days, from 7 till 1 the next morning, dancing, laughing, shouting, and screaming, and having the most emotional experience I've ever had in my life. So, although I was ecstatic, I was also quite emotionally drained, and I had a thumping headache. The old me would have gone to bed, but as I had just spent the last 4 days listening to Tony tell me I needed to take action, action, action, there was no way on earth I was going to go and lie down in bed, with all this new knowledge buzzing around my head!

One of my fears, or anxieties if you like, was walking my greyhound. He caused me a huge amount of stress, as he would be extremely reactive to any dog he saw in the distance, and he would look very aggressive. We were not able to get close to other dogs, or walk along the same street, which made walking him very stressful, and I would often get in a complete state, with lots of tears. With my newfound knowledge, I decided to take immediate action the moment I got home, even with my thumping headache. I harnessed up George, my greyhound, and put his muzzle on, and then I took him straight to the local field. I used my new knowledge that I had learnt on how to control my emotions while I was doing this scary task. Instead of focusing on the fears and the anxiety of what would happen if another dog came along, I used Tony's techniques and changed my focus, body language, and my internal language to myself. This, of course, made a dramatic change. George and I walked down the alley, which normally caused me a huge amount of anxiety, and into the field. I felt a great sense of achievement and freedom; plus, I was very proud of myself!

> *"Opportunities don't happen. You create them."*
> – Chris Grosser

Tony Robbins taught me not to listen to excuses, as your excuses are just your fear talking. Each day after the seminar, I took more and more action. I cannot stress how important momentum is when building confidence and self-esteem. If you are going to invest in a coach or somebody with more experience and knowledge in a subject than yourself, then it makes sense to not only listen to that expert but to put their words into action.

> *"The only place where success comes before work is in the dictionary."*
> – Vidal Sassoon

Each day, I listened to Tony on YouTube, and to my heartbeat music, to continue with my motivated, happy, positive feelings that I had generated, and I kept the momentum going. This is so important, especially at the very beginning when it is so easy to slip back into old habits. I am not suggesting that it is easy for everyone to change their emotions in 4 days, and that this will last for good—it takes hard work, determination, and effort.

> *"It does not matter how slowly you go, so long as you do not stop."*
> – Confucius

When you have spent years with a negative dialog, it takes time to reverse that, but it is so worth it. Tony taught me the six human needs, and on the occasional down day—because I did have them—I would go back to my notepad and look over these needs, and see which one I was lacking to be creating the feeling that I was feeling at the time. On days that I was sucked into a depression again, I was able to pull out my notepad and use the knowledge that I had learnt, to write down the 4 human needs and the two spiritual needs, and attempt to find out how I was not meeting those at the time. I remember one day when big teardrops were splashing onto my paper as I cried my way through writing down my needs. By the end of the task, it was clear that I was not loving myself enough, and that is why I had slipped back into my depression. Depression was my default love pattern. I found that the 6 human needs were fascinating to learn, and they truly did, and still do, help me to live a healthy, happy, mentally balanced life.

So, how did I change my life? I took advice from someone who knew, I put it into action, and I kept the momentum going. It is not easy, but it is as simple as that.

Freedom and Inner Confidence

It is difficult to explain how I feel now, and I think you may only understand if you have been suffering yourself for many years. The only way I can describe how I used to feel is if you imagine carrying around a heavy rucksack, wearing headphones and blinkers, with the constant feeling of a black cloud hanging over your head. Now, the rucksack has been put down, the earphones and blinkers taken off, and that cloud of dread has drifted far away. I feel free. Those simple three words do not do it justice, but they completely sum up how I feel each day: free to live my life how I wish to live it; free to say the things that I wish to say; free to step out of the house when I want to; free to achieve my dreams; and most importantly, free to feel the way I want to feel. You can only understand this sheer glory of freedom when you have not had it for so long. The chains of anxiety that were wrapped around me have now been unshackled, and I am free to live the life I was born to live.

> *"It's fine to celebrate success,*
> *but it is more important to heed the lessons of failure."*
> *– Bill Gates*

If you are reading this book, and you are experiencing any kind of suffering, then I urge you to keep on reading, take the action, and keep the momentum going, so you too can feel the sheer joy of freedom that can and will come to you in reward for your hard work. Don't get used to how you feel; don't accept it and say that it's just your personality. If it's something that is making you unhappy, then it can and must be changed. I used to think that being anxious and unconfident was just my personality: You are just shy; you're a quiet kind of girl. Conscientious was a word often used in my school reports. There is a big difference between being a quiet, conscientious, happy person, and being a quiet, conscientious, anxious, unconfident person. I will never be the life and soul of a party, I will never be the loudest person in a room, and I will never be a social butterfly—and I don't want to be. I am quite happy being a quiet kind of person, but now I am a quietly confident kind of person. I don't need the world to know that I am confident. If I feel it myself, that is all I need.

> "It's all about confidence and how you feel about yourself. There's no such thing as a perfect woman. I like imperfections—that's what makes you unique."
> – Hayley Hasselhoff

I think, sometimes, if you are a quiet person, you worry about becoming overly confident and then looking cocky or obnoxious. I hope that by me writing this book, you can see that it is possible to go from no confidence and no self-esteem, to a quiet confidence that gives you inner peace and happiness. You do not need to be the bold, flashy, loud one (unless you want to be). I feel there are many books out there on confidence that are written by people who have never experienced the pain or lack of no confidence. I hope, with my knowledge and experience of the struggles, that I can help you and your child to take the small steps needed to build you up, knowing exactly how you will be feeling along the way.

The Birth of the Motivated Mummies

The most amazing effect that I have seen whilst starting my self-development is not in myself. The difference it has made to my children and my family home is much greater than I ever imagined. I thought, by changing myself, I would purely change how I felt, but by changing myself, I have changed the whole world around me, including my family. This is how *Motivated Mummies* developed. Seeing the huge change in my children, from my own development, has encouraged me to help other mothers to grow within their own lives, so that they too can help impact on their children in a positive way. We don't always realise the effect that we have on our children, but believe me, it is huge.

My youngest daughter used to suffer with anxiety, and I felt incredibly guilty that I had passed this on to her, thinking that it was hereditary. My dad had depression, I had depression, and now she had it, so it was easy to understand why I thought it was hereditary. The harsh truth is that it is a learnt behaviour—no child is born depressed. I know there have been studies to show that babies pick up on the emotions and feelings of their mother while in the womb, and that babies also pick up on emotions around them once they are born. This does not mean that a baby or young child is clinically depressed; it means that these are emotions they've grown used to. What is the quickest way to help an infant out of low mood? By helping the mother change her emotions and feelings, so that her energy that she is passing on to her child is positive and beneficial.

I still can't believe the benefits that have come from my new attitude, and the difference it has made to my children. It's just huge, especially to my youngest daughter, who I'm guessing was at a more impressionable age when I started. Again, this emphasizes my reasons for wanting more mothers to be aware of their behaviour and the effects it has on their children. My youngest was 9 when I first took hold of my own life and started living by design and not on default mode.

I remember one day when she was setting the table for dinner, and we, as a family, were manifesting my dream partner. "Do you want me to set a place for your boyfriend, Mummy?" she asked. "No darling," I replied. "We're not crazy." Bless her; we had already pulled the table away from the wall to sit a fourth seat down, made space in my wardrobe for his clothes, and made both girls sit in the back of the car to keep the front passenger space clear for him, but setting a place at the table was crazy? We had gone well past crazy! More about this later….

"The true sign of intelligence is not knowledge but imagination."
– Albert Einstein

My children had spent the first 9 and 12 years of their lives listening to me moan, complain, and see the glass as half empty. Of course, I did not do all this in front of them on purpose, but little bits slip out when this is your natural disposition. I could easily spend the rest of the book beating myself up over how I raised them and what I could have done better, but at the time, I was doing my best. With everything I was going through, and all the tools and knowledge I had at the time, I was doing my very best. That is a very important lesson to learn. We, and everyone else, can only do what we know to do. Even if we sat and debated each situation for hours on end, we would end up doing the best we knew to do. We simply cannot do any better than our best at each time. Take a minute to think of someone who may have harmed you in the past. What actions did they take? They were only doing what they knew to do. This could be completely inadequate in your eyes, but every person has their own set of beliefs, values, and morals, and they are all different. Just because your values are higher, or you know better than they do, it does not mean that they didn't do the best of their ability at that moment.

> "To effectively communicate, we must realize that we are all different in the way we perceive the world, and use this understanding as a guide to our communication with others."
> – Tony Robbins

I was in a session the other day, and a client said that she often forgives peoples actions, and says, "It's not their fault that they are stupid." This made me laugh. It is a little harsh, but if it helps to see it like that, then why not. You could say that when I was raising my children, I was stupid. I treated them like friends rather than parenting them. Was I stupid or simply doing what I knew at the time?

This concept really helped with my own issues with people who had hurt me in the past. Yes, they treated me badly, but were they just doing what they knew to do, and what their beliefs, morals, and values dictated? People behave differently because they have different standards and beliefs. We are all just trying to do what we feel is best, and we are all surviving the only way we know how—as was I, as are you. We can choose to continue to just survive, or we can choose to grow and develop. I am glad I am on the road to higher personal development, as it certainly brings more happiness to myself and everyone I meet. Don't waste time wishing people were different, or wishing your actions had been different, or wishing things hadn't happened. People are what they are, and things have happened to each one of us. Now we must pick ourselves up, dust ourselves off, and learn and grow so we can be our best selves.

> "Learn from yesterday, live for today, hope for tomorrow. The important thing is not to stop questioning."
> – Albert Einstein

I am teaching myself to be my best self, and whilst I am doing that, my girls are watching. I have said many times that our children don't often do as we say, but they do watch what we do, and they do copy us. My girl's personal growth has been huge over the last few years. They have grown in confidence, self-love, and maturity beyond their years. Of course, I have tried to coach them, but I'm not perfect; I'm still a pushy mum every now and then. Now and then is better than 24/7, so I let myself off and don't beat myself up about it (that's their job). I send them YouTube videos that I'm sure they just delete; I give them words of encouragement that they roll their eyes at, and I offer to help them at their times of struggle. Do they let me? No way, never! So, I walk away, and I go "fix" myself instead, but they see this. They see me cooking dinner and watching motivational videos on YouTube; they see me studying new knowledge and always learning even though I'm old (to them); they see me take time out of my busy day to go to yoga classes; and they see me spend time and money on myself and my personal health and wellbeing. I am doing what I want them to do. We want our children to know they are important and worth investing in, so we must demonstrate that ourselves.

I had been asking them to try my health smoothies, and every now and then they would take a sip. A year on, and they have both swapped their cereals for healthy breakfast smoothies or a nutritious meal! I am over the moon. If I had stopped making mine and gone back to cereals, they never would have made the change. Now they start the day with the best nutrition to keep their energy high, rather than a sugar high, which would be followed by a sugar low. They have even started their own workouts together, and added in some yoga moves. They are learning that healthy eating and exercise is vital to your overall wellbeing. If I was feeling too guilty spending money on healthy foods or yoga classes, this very positive change would not have occurred for my children. It is more selfish NOT to spend time effort and money on yourself, and while many mums feel too guilty to do this, they should in fact feel guilty for not doing it. By denying yourself this healthy lifestyle, you deny your child the role model they need to learn from.

Later in the book, you will read testimonials from ladies in all walks of life, on how their confidence improved by changing their eating or starting an exercise plan. I wonder if you will be able to relate to one of their stories.

Wonder Woman

People have asked me why I wanted to start my coaching business, and why *The Motivated Mummies*. Having been a mum for 19 years, 8 of those as a single mum, I have seen the change in my children due to my own transformation. Being a nursery manager, and seeing child development with many different children, I can honestly say, as we all know, children are the development of the parents or of their significant adult that raised them.

In my coaching practice, I have many women come to me with concerns for their children, about their lack of confidence, anxiety issues, and a lack of drive in their teenagers. They ask me if I can help their child. When I came into coaching, it was never my aim to work with children again. I love the proactive side of coaching, and I love the action plans and the drive, but I felt that children were so much more complex, and I couldn't get the results I wanted with them—I was so wrong! Having worked with a variety of teenagers and younger children, I can say they are not that different, and they can be just as driven and just as motivated as any adult—even more so sometimes. My problem is that we have a fantastic session, and then the parent arrives to collect them, and they make one comment that makes me want to hit my head against the wall! Internally, I am thinking, "How can I possibly help this child when they are on a river that is flowing in a different direction. That child must be one strong, determined little cookie to paddle upstream while the rest of the family are flowing down stream."

I try my best to encourage the parents to have at least one conversation with me, if not a few sessions. Some do, and this is so much more constructive to the child's success; success being whatever the child/family are trying to achieve, which is usually happiness, confidence, or a reduction in anxiety. Of course, the parent never sees this issue; they think it is the child's problem, and once that is solved, everything will be rosy. Sadly, this is not usually the case. There is a reason the child is unhappy, anxious, or unconfident, and although therapy is FANTASTIC for the child, family therapy or coaching for the parent is paramount. Even as adults, we still aim to please our parents, so if your child thinks they need to be a certain way to receive love from you or to please you, they will act accordingly to get that. You won't necessarily be able to see this, but a professional looking in can spot it clearly; but once you know, you can change your habits to best help your child. This is why I set up The Motivated Mummies.

I strongly believe that the mother figure in the household is the glue of the family. Women are extremely strong, and we have an inner unique quality that keeps us going when times are tough. We do what needs to be done, simply because it needs to be done. We put others before ourselves daily, and we have a strong urge to protect and to nurture. You've heard the saying, *"happy wife, happy life."* That saying is there for a reason: If the woman of the household is happy, then the rest of the household is happy. She is the one that gives off the most energy to the rest of the family, and she is the one that everybody looks up to, whether they realise it or not.

We all need and crave the love of our parents and, fundamentally, everything we do is to please them. I've been in numerous coaching sessions, and the one thing that always comes up constantly is the person's childhood. Regardless of how old they are, their childhood always comes up, along with their parents. Imagine if all mums had the knowledge, the power, and the strategies to create confidence within their children, balance within their lifestyles, strong and healthy relationships, and a guilt-free way of living! Imagine what that family unit would look like if that was all in place. I strongly believe that with these four categories, we can create unstoppable incredible families. Families have cycles that tend to repeat themselves, generation after generation, and if we could just break that cycle, then we could start to create new cycles of positive, healthy, motivated children, who would then go on to have positive, healthy, motivated children, and thus the new cycle starts to appear. In my opinion, the only way we can do that is by breaking the pattern somewhere, and because the mum is usually the one in charge of the household, by tackling her beliefs, and her way of living and thinking, I believe that is the quickest way to filter down to the whole family. Once the mother has learnt these techniques and these ideas, she not only can make herself happier, but she will then, naturally and by default, be a great role model to her children, and they will naturally copy. If she has a partner, these will slowly rub off on her partner as well.

Once the mum has gained the knowledge and the power, she is then able to use that to break other family members' patterns. She could even use this with in-laws, at her workplace, teaching her children how to do it at their schools—the opportunities are endless. Most women are so strong and so determined, and so dedicated to their children that they will do literally anything that they feel is right to protect their child and to help them in the future, so giving women these ideas and new strategies in the first place is the perfect way to help them to empower their own families.

> *"Life is a gift, and it offers us the privilege, opportunity, and responsibility to give something back by becoming more."*
> – Tony Robbins

ACTION

Answer the following questions as honestly as you can to start creating your own action plan.

- Who are you?
- What are your core beliefs and values?
- Do you have a story you tell yourself and others?
- Is this story holding you back?
- Are you a great role model to your child?
- Are you happy with yourself?
- Could improving yourself benefit your child?
- Are you ready to be open to learning new skills?

Notes

Chapter 2

What Is Confidence?

Step 1: Identify the Problem

As a society, we tend to have a stereotypical view of confidence and what it looks like. If someone walks into a room, head held high, and speaking loudly and being the dominate figure, we assume they are confident. Then we may see a person sitting on their own, head down, reading a book, away from everyone else, and we assume they are too shy to join in. In reality, the loud person could be desperately trying to hide their lack of confidence, and the quiet person may have an inner confidence, and does not need to be the loudest person in the room.

What is confidence, and can we really label ourselves as confident or not confident? Surely, we all have different levels of confidence in different areas of our lives. For example, you may be highly confident in your workplace, well respected, and not afraid to speak your mind, but put you in front of your mother-in-law, and you're a quivering mess, unable to put your point of view across. It is incorrect to label yourself when there are so many different areas. Give yourself credit where credit is due, and accept that you have confidence in some areas, and that you need to grow and build your confidence in others. By saying this, it automatically boosts your confidence to know that it can be achieved. Don't worry if you feel you do not have enough confidence in any area of your life; it just means we can build on all of it in one go, and concentrate on acceptance.

Take a minute to think where your strengths and weaknesses truly are. Do you feel you are a good mother? Do you feel you are good at keeping the home nice? Do you feel like you are a great career woman? Do you feel confident in your ability to be a fantastic wife or partner? Are you a great daughter or friend? Are you confident in your ability to be organised and prepared? Don't be quick to label yourselves as lacking in confidence, as when you really think about it, there are many areas that you are striving in, but the reason you don't think about these is because they don't bother you, so you don't linger on the thoughts, and you don't focus on it.

I have always prided myself on being a good mother, and the reason for this was that I had evidence. When I felt I lacked confidence in absolutely everything else, I had evidence that my parenting skills were good, as my children had turned out well in my opinion—but you shouldn't use evidence as a way of gauging your ability. By allowing evidence to control you, you are putting your happiness in somebody else's hands, as everyone has a different reality, and one person's evidence is different from another's. It was not long ago that I felt I had failed as a parent, simply because both children in one evening were not happy with their lives. One evening out of 16 years, where they both were not happy at the same time, and all of a sudden, I let go of my confidence of being a good parent, because the evidence pointed to my failings. I was allowing somebody else, or in this case, two other people, to dictate my own feelings and my ability, where in truth, they just both happened to be having a bad day at the same time, and my energy must have also been low to allow that to have affected me so badly. If my self-esteem had been high that day, it would have been water off a duck's back, and I would have known that it would all blow over in a couple of hours, as it did. But as I was feeling particularly insignificant in another area of my life, I allowed this incident to affect me more than it should have. This is the danger

What Is Confidence?

of allowing evidence to gauge your ability. Your own ability in something is your own opinion, and nobody else has a right to say whether it's good enough or not. After all, what is ever good enough? This is different for different people.

What does confidence look like to you? As I just said, we all have different opinions on everything, so whose opinion are you trying to live up to in regard to your confidence? Before you can learn to be more confident, you need to learn what this looks like to you. What would it look like to be more confident in the different areas of your life? If you had confidence at work, what does that look like? Would you be able to speak to groups of people without rehearsing beforehand? Would you be able to put your point across easily and clearly? Would you submit ideas to the boss rather than holding them back? What exactly would you do differently at work if you had more confidence? You need to get very specific, because it's all too easy to just say, "Oh, I just don't have confidence at work." If you don't get specific, you won't know what you want, and then you won't know how to change it. By determining what it is that you would like to be doing differently, you can then take small action steps to achieving that.

The same goes for every area of your life that you would like to build confidence in. If you would like confidence in social situations, what does that look like to you? Would it mean walking out of your house without worrying what you look like? Would it mean walking into a shop and smiling, and looking at the cashier in the eyes? Maybe it would mean asking for an item that you could not see on display. It could mean walking into the pub and feeling like you belong there, feeling comfortable in what you're wearing, and that you look good. Be absolutely specific. This could be a very long list for some people, or it could just be one or two points for others; and what some can do easily, others may find really hard. Don't beat yourself up over your list; just be proud you are taking action.

For me, when I had social phobia and anxiety, my list would have been huge. I did not feel comfortable in my own skin, so no matter what I wore, I didn't feel like I looked good enough. It didn't matter where I went; I didn't feel like I belonged. And it didn't matter who I was around; I didn't feel like I was on their wavelength. I am living proof that even if you are this extreme, you can still turn your life around. Steps can be taken to enable you to feel differently. You just have to want it badly enough to take the action. It's not about being a completely different person; it's just feeling comfortable in those situations. You do not have to all of a sudden be the life and soul of the party, or be a cocky salesperson at your company. You just have to feel quietly confident, knowing it's okay to be you, and it's okay to do what you want to do.

I was at the supermarket the other day, and a lady was trying to get some squeezy yogurts out of the box on the shelf. The box was sealed shut, and someone had obviously forgotten to break it open. She gave a couple of attempts and then gave up. I felt sorry for her as she clearly wanted the yogurts, and going by the type they were, she needed them for her children. As I stood next to her, I wondered if I was making her feel judged, so I said, "Go on, rip it open," to lighten the mood. She laughed and tried again with no luck. Having been in that situation so many times, I knew how disappointed she would be with herself when she got home, or when it came to packing the lunch box the next day, so I said, "Here, let me try." I continued to hack at the box until it was open, and we joked about breaking a nail (She had lovely nails, and mine were stubby, unpolished ones.), but we got the yogurts loose, and she walked away happy.

This was one little incident where lack of confidence could have made her give up. You may say it's not the end of the world, but when those incidents mount up, that is your world. It's a world of mini disappointments and tiny failures. These slowly but surely knock your confidence and your self-esteem. That's why I'll be teaching you that little action steps, like getting yogurt off a shelf, all work wonders to building up your self-esteem.

Of course, I still have times when I lack confidence. It's only natural, especially as I am continuing to grow and develop myself. I have times of self-doubt and worry, and times when I don't feel like I'm good enough to achieve what I want to. This is all a lack of confidence and a lack of self-belief. The difference between now and the old days is, I don't stay there! I don't stay with that belief, and I don't allow it to rule my life. I now know that I can change that feeling, because it is just a feeling; it is not my life. So, I go by the rules I'm telling you today. I listen to my story, I decide what I need to do to gain confidence in the area that I'm worried about, and I seek out the knowledge that I need to move me forward; whether that be going on a course, watching some YouTube clips, or phoning up a coach and working through it on a one to one, breaking down what's really bothering me. Taking action is one of the most important things that you can do to build confidence; not accepting that this is how it is, but knowing that you can do something to change and to better it. Learning that I am in control of my life is the most important thing that I have ever learnt. You are in control of your life. You can change anything that you are not happy with, and you can do this by either changing the circumstance or changing your feelings toward it.

Confidence Comes with Age

I have heard many people say that confidence comes with age. This annoys me on two parts. One, do we really have to wait until we are 40, 50, or 60, before we have the confidence to tell someone what we think? Let's face it; that is what they are talking about when they say confidence comes with age. They mean when old people just blurt out whatever they are thinking, with no thought for other people. We've all seen these kinds of people, and those who go out without brushing their hair because they don't care what other people think about them anymore. Well, just hold on a minute, and let's think about that. If you thought having confidence means that you are mean to people or come across as rude, or if it symbolises walking through the town looking like you've been dragged through a hedge backwards, are you really going to want to become confident? I think not. You may not consciously think these thoughts to yourself, but unconsciously, on a much deeper level, it could be a massive block from wanting to become more confident.

I heard a beautiful story from a client about her 8-year-old son, which blows this "confidence comes with age" miff out of the water. He was in class one day, and his teacher had been feeling poorly with a sore throat. They had a substitute teacher the day before, as his teacher could not speak. The children in his class were being particularly noisy, and the teacher was struggling to gain the attention of the class. Satinderpal stood up and shouted to the whole class, "Hey, be quiet everyone! Don't you know Miss Walker can't speak?" The class fell silent, and the authoritative voice the child had used forced each class member to consider their actions and remain silent for the rest of the lesson.

This story did not surprise me at all! Both Satinderpal's parents hold roles of authority in their careers, and this action is very much something that they would have done themselves. As his mum relayed the story, she told me as if it was normal for an eight-year-old to stand up against his friends and take such action. She even went on to say she asked him why he didn't add something else before he sat down! It was expected of him. This confident action was expected.

Maybe when we have children, we don't expect them to be confident, so without realising it, we do little things for them to save them the pressure or stress of having to do it. But all we are really doing is teaching our children that it's okay not to have confidence now, and that they can have that later when they are older. I know for a fact that I felt this way about my children. I tarred them with the same brush as myself. If I was not confident to do it, then how could they possibly be asked to do it?

I have also met many older people who are severely lacking in confidence, and this stereotypical idea that you get confidence as you get older only damages their self-esteem even more, making them feel alienated and abnormal. The truth of the matter is that age has nothing at all to do with our confidence, but it could be that as we have got older, we have learnt more.

Your WHY

One of the things that will help you along the way is to know your WHY. In coaching, we speak of your WHY a lot, as it helps to keep you on track with any goal. Ask yourself, why do you want to do this? Whom are you doing this for? Who will benefit from the new improved you, and who is watching you and your behaviour right now? Who will be watching you grow in confidence, learning the skills that you will be teaching them just by being the new improved you? It is very important to know your WHY, as there will be times when this fight will feel too hard, and you will want to take the easy option and not stand up for yourself and not move forward with your growth. Remembering your WHY, and remembering whom you're doing this for, and what benefits you will get from it, will help to push you through the tough times. Sometimes we need to acknowledge what we are doing to our loved ones around us, to give us the push we need to make the change. How is your lack of confidence affecting your family and your loved ones now? How is it affecting your friends, and how is it affecting your personal health and wellbeing?

We sometimes forget to think of others, and feel that it is only ourselves that it is hurting. For example, when you put on a dress and then beat yourself up because you do not look as perfect as you think you should, who is that affecting? You may think it's just affecting you, but if you are standing in front of a mirror, saying out loud that your bum looks too big, or your boobs are too small, or your thighs are too fat for these jeans, and you have your daughter playing on the floor next to you, she can hear you saying those words. She's taking it in, whether she realises it or not, and if these words are what she hears on a regular basis, she will also grow up to believe that she is not good enough—her body may be too fat, or her bottom too big, or her boobs too small. If she hears the one person that she trusts the most in the world saying that they are not good enough, when in her eyes you look amazing, what is that going to do for her own body image as she grows up? Do you want your children to get dressed in the morning and feel that they are not perfect, or do you want your children to get dressed knowing that they are unique and special, and valuable and loved! It doesn't matter if they have a bit of cellulite, or if they have a few spots, or if their bottom is not the right size or the perfect shape that society says it should be. Do you want them to be focusing on that, or do you want them to be focusing on their health, their happiness, and their fulfilment?

What about when you turn your friends down because you don't have the confidence to go out and meet them in the pub? What if your friend needed to talk to you that night, and she felt rejected because you've turned her down for the 10th time that month? When you look at it like that, it really is quite selfish, and your confidence issue is affecting many people.

How about the added pressure on your partner to keep lifting you up and telling you that you look good, and that you are worthy enough? People can only take things for so long before they get deflated themselves. I had a client who came to me and said her husband had had an affair, and she was so angry that he could do such a thing. I had to bite my tongue because, for the past 4 weeks that I had known her, I had heard how she constantly told him that she was ugly and not good enough. She told me how he used to praise her all the time and say how pretty she was, but she would tell him that he was wrong, and I thought to myself that it must be so draining for him. To keep on reassuring her, and to be told his opinion didn't matter and he was wrong, what does that also say about him, and his taste in women? As harsh as it sounds, I was not surprised that he had found somebody to give him some attention and share his love with. So, stop and look at whose life you are affecting with your lack of confidence, and whose life you could improve if you improved your own. Use this information to write your WHY, and make it strong and powerful, and this will help to drive you forward.

ACTION

- In which areas of your life would you like to improve your confidence?
- What would this look like to you?
- What is your WHY?

Notes

Chapter 3

Knowledge Is Power

Step 2: Educate Yourself

Do you remember your first day of nursery school, standing at the big school gate, holding your mum's hand, waiting with nervous excitement to go in? You didn't know what to expect, and you didn't know what to do once you entered the big colourful room. It was probably a little bit overwhelming. Were you supposed to go and put your lunchbox away first, or did you hang your coat up? Where should your coat go, and which peg was yours? Were you supposed to go and play, or did you sit straight down on the mat? On your very first day, you had all these questions, so you probably weren't feeling very confident. But look what happened. The teacher sat you down on the mat, and she explained what you should be doing when you first come into the nursery. Walking you through your day—explaining which peg was yours and where to hang your coat, and to put your snack box on the trolley and come and sit down on the mat—the instructions were very clear. So, the next day, standing at the big gate, you may have had a thousand thoughts flash through your mind, but you knew exactly what you were supposed to do when you walked in the doors, and this gave you much more confidence in walking in.

Do you remember riding a bike for the first time, or going to swimming lessons? Generally, we all need to be shown how to do these activities.

Some of us may only need to be shown once or twice, while others need months of training, but we are taught to sit on the bike, hold the handlebars, put our feet on the pedals, and pedal like crazy! When you stop pedalling, put your feet down before you fall off—simple instructions. All we had to do is go practice. I remember my swimming lessons at school quite vividly because I hated them, and the thought of having to get undressed in front of everybody, and stand around in front of the boys, in my swimming costume, when I was a chubby little thing, did not fill me with happiness. I remember one specific incident where Mr Sahota held my feet as I was doing the backstroke, and he was telling me that if I moved my arms hard enough, I would keep my head above the water—I remember swallowing quite a bit that day. The certificate I was aiming for was my confidence certificate. They called it that because it was when you reached a level of confidence within the water. You could swim by yourself, having learnt what to do, but you hadn't put it into action much yet; and that's what it's all about, isn't it? Being told what to do, and then putting it into action. I think we sometimes forget as adults that we still need to learn things, and we are sometimes too hard on ourselves and expect everything to come naturally to us.

> *"Insanity: Doing the same thing over and over again and expecting different results."*
> – Albert Einstein

There are many different areas that you could feel confidence or lack of confidence in, and you have two options in life: You can carry on your journey, feeling a lack of confidence, or you can seek out a way to build your confidence in that area. As I have already mentioned, I suffered with social phobia, which meant I could not speak in public easily. With 3 or more people, my hearing seemed to shut off, my legs would turn to jelly, and for some reason, I would go mute. I may have 1000 things that I would like to contribute to the conversation, but for some reason, they just would not come out of my mouth. I spent all my school life like this, so I do feel like I missed out on a large chunk of social skills as I was growing up, and I still feel like I'm behind everybody else in that department. After attending UPW (Unleash the Power Within), and regaining control of my life and letting go, I decided I wanted to take it one step further (being the determined person that I am). I wanted to be able to speak confidently in public, whether this be in a work capacity, in front of groups of people, or just in a social capacity, down at the pub, in front of my friends. I wanted to feel confident to just speak, something I had never felt before, not as far as I can remember. I spoke with my coach about this issue, and he told me of a group called Toastmasters. It was an international group, and I was sure to have one nearby me somewhere, so I looked it up. Sure enough, there were two local groups not far away. I went along one day to see what it would be like, and I was very surprised at how organised and well run it was. I suppose I was expecting it to be more of a laid-back, half-hearted event. I was very happy to see that it all ran to time, and there was a proper format to be followed. Everyone there was so friendly, and made me feel very welcome, but I still felt terrified.

I had gotten over my generalised anxiety, but speaking in front of a group of strangers is a scary thought for most people. I was very proud of myself as I volunteered to do what is called table topics, which means that I was asked a question and had to stand up at the front and speak about the question for up to 2 minutes. I think I managed 1 minute, but I managed it nevertheless. The hardest thing I found was the break time, when people were just mingling and chatting casually. I had always struggled with break times at school. I just never knew what to say, and was never brave enough to join in. Who was I to go up to somebody and just stand next to them and wait to join in their conversation? Was I even worthy of doing that? Even after UPW, my confidence wasn't rock solid. Plus, I would much rather have a deep and meaningful discussion on someone's hopes and dreams than talk about something casual like the weather. As time passed, and I continued to go back to Toastmasters, I started to feel more and more relaxed in the situation, and I was even able to go up to people and start a conversation.

> *"If you do what you've always done,
> you'll get what you've always gotten."*
> – Tony Robbins

The idea of this book is to explain how, and to guide you into feeling more confident, so I will tell you exactly how I was able to start small talk with the guys at Toastmasters. It feels a little embarrassing to say, but I actually Googled small talk. I looked up conversation starters, and I spoke to my partner for ideas on what I could say to people, and I asked my friends on Facebook. If these things don't come naturally to you, then what else are you supposed to do but learn them from somebody who they do come naturally to? So, I made a mental note of some awesome conversation starters, and I slowly put them into practice at my toastmaster group. I'm sure they did not come out awesome, but it was not long before it started to become more natural, and I didn't need to think about it so much.

In regard to the actual speeches, I could put my name down to do a structured speech anytime I wanted. These would last between 5 and 7 minutes—no, I'm not going to tell you that I'm a pro, but I can definitely tell you that I am getting better. When I suffered from social phobia, I could not look anybody in the eye when I was speaking to them. This all changed as I became more confident, but once again, as I stood up in front of the group at Toastmasters to do my structured speech, it all came flooding back. All the old fears of what people would think of me—who was I to be standing up there, and why should they be listening to me in the first place—all these fears brought back my anxiety. I felt that if I did not look at them, they would not be able to see me. I know that sounds crazy, but fear has no logic. I was elated with the last speech I did at Toastmasters. It was not perfect by any stretch of the imagination, but it involved interaction, and I managed to look at many people in the eye—I was very proud of myself! So, the moral of this story is, it doesn't matter how difficult you find something; you can always better yourself at it by learning from those who know, and putting it into practice. I am so grateful for the Toastmasters gang, and for Raphael for telling me about it, as on February 23rd, 2019, I was able to stand up at my own wedding and say a speech in front of my 80 guests. I had written the speech in my head, on my drive over to my mums, and I wrote it down the next day, and read it the morning of the wedding, and that was it!! I remember walking into the wedding breakfast with Steve, now my husband, saying, "Steve, I haven't learnt my speech!" But I took a deep breath, looked at all my friends and family, and as much as I could, I used my new Toastmaster skills to present a speech I was very proud of. I now have absolutely no regrets about that day, as I know I would have been disappointed if I hadn't done it. One day, I may be a professional speaker—you never know. From social phobia and mute, to speaking on a stage in front of thousands; now, there's a thought….

Learn and Grow

Learning something new is one of the best things you can do to build your confidence, whether this be learning something specifically that will help build your confidence in that area, or learning something completely disassociated to it. For example, if you have a fear of social speaking, and you went and learnt belly dancing, this would not help improve your knowledge of small talk; but it would help your small talk, as you would have something fun and exciting to talk about when you met people. Learning something new and fun also increases your confidence because it boosts your self-esteem and increases natural serotonin in your brain. This serotonin helps increase thought patterns and creativity, relieves anxiety, gives better sleep, and is a great mood booster. Serotonin is known as the feel-good hormone, and it is a natural antidepressant.

There are many classes available for you to attend these days. They range from high-end workshops, focusing on teaching you lifelong lessons and giving practical advice and knowledge that can benefit your everyday life and your career, to weekly workshops on a range of different topics, all the way down to taster sessions and free events held locally by the community, all of which will benefit your overall well-being, and promote confidence in yourself. If you are struggling to find events, check out Eventbrite, Facebook events, and go to your local library, churches, and community halls. Also, the doctor's surgery often has posters displayed in social groups that could benefit you. Not only will you learn a new skill, promote natural serotonin in your body, and boost your mood, you will also meet new friends and associates, which is just as important.

When I was in my late 20s, I decided to go back to college and study, as I was no longer happy being the manager of a day nursery. I studied every Monday evening whilst working all week with two young children. It wasn't easy, and I definitely could not have done it without the help of my mum. She babysat for me every Monday evening, but it was something I felt that I needed to do, and I truly believe it is never too late to change your career. We are at work for longer than we are doing anything else, and I really do believe that we need to be happy in our work, and that way we give our best to our colleagues, clients, and ourselves. So, I went back to college as a mature student, and I thoroughly enjoyed the two years that I spent there, training to become a beautician and a masseuse. This whole process of going back to college really did help to boost my confidence at the time. I was surrounded by people who wanted to learn, people who were interested in the same things as me, and who were happy to grow and better themselves. These are the kind of people you really need to be surrounding yourself with. I also made a good friend at college, and 12 years later, we are still friends. You never know whom you're going to meet along the journey of life, but if you don't get out there and do new things, your chances of meeting amazing people will dramatically reduce, and that would be a great shame. I personally have met some amazing people by doing activities that were well out of my comfort zone.

*"Successful people ask better questions,
and as a result, they get better answers."*
– Tony Robbins

So, what could you do to boost your confidence? What could you study that would help you? Would it be a fun topic, such as belly dancing or ballroom dancing? What about trampolining? Is there a group that you could join with your child, and do it together? This would be fantastic, as it would help for many different reasons: First, you would be educating yourself, which we have already discussed the benefits of; second, you would not have to find a babysitter or a time when you did not have your child; third, your child would be gaining all the benefits that we have just discussed, and building their confidence, regardless if they need it or not (you can never be too confident in life); and fourth, it would be fantastic quality time for you and your child. These are the kinds of things that children look back on and remember in their childhood, much more than an expensive gift that you've struggled to pay for. What is life about if not having as many experiences as possible while we're here?

I wonder if you could plan 2 activities—one for both of you, and one for you alone. These do not have to be ongoing courses. I booked my daughter and myself for a cupcake-making day once. We went separately, as she did not want to go when I booked it the first time, but when I returned home, telling her how much fun I'd had making cupcakes that look like a bouquet of flowers, she was much more open to go the next time, so when the opportunity arose again, I booked for her and her friend to go along, and this time they made cakes with unicorns and rainbows. It was out of her comfort zone, and she was surrounded by people she did not know, but she had a great time, and that would have boosted her confidence a lot. There are many fun activities that pop-up, and they could just be a couple of hours long. You do not have to do courses that take 6 months, but you can if you want to. We are very lucky to have so many opportunities around us at the moment. Even if we cannot get out of the house, there are many online courses that are not expensive at all, and a lot of these courses involve community groups; so you apply for an online course, and they automatically add you into the community of everybody else who is attending that course. So, even if you cannot get out of the house, you can still be part of a community and grow and learn. This will boost your confidence, and there really are no excuses—there is something for everybody out there.

I have many clients who attend sewing sessions, arts and crafts events, and book and poetry writing, and they always have something to say. It's so interesting to hear what they've been up to, and what they learnt last week. If they had chosen not to take on those events and activities, what would they have to say when they saw their friends next time—that they had sat and watched countdown again for the 5th time that week? That would not boost their confidence or their self-esteem. Get out there, have a look at what you can do, and join in. I highly recommend you doing something by yourself, because it opens you up to meeting lots more people. If you go to an event with a friend, the chances of you talking to others are already dramatically reduced. Go to events by yourself, and people will come up and talk to you. It will also give you the push to go and speak to other people. It may be uncomfortable to start with, but over time, your confidence will grow, and you'll feel much better about going to new places by yourself. We often tell our children to go to lunchtime clubs, weekend clubs, etc., but maybe we should just lead by example.

When my children were little, I never made them queue up by themselves to pay for anything. As a shy and unconfident child, I would never ever do that myself, so I wouldn't ask them to go and do something that I wouldn't do. I didn't ask them to do very much, because I assumed that they would feel as uncomfortable as I did. I can now see, looking back, that this was the wrong thing to do, because all I was doing was teaching them to be scared of stepping out of their comfort zone. I remember that my comfort zone was pretty much curled up in bed under my duvet—not very big at all. Your actions are what you truly teach your children. It doesn't matter what you say to them; it's what you do that they copy. So, if your child sees you going out at night to an evening class, you should not feel guilty for leaving them, but proud that you are showing them how to live a confident, fulfilled life. If you have spent some quality time with them that day, they will grow up knowing that they too should step out of their comfort zone and learn and grow. You will be much more able to convince them to take up a class themselves if they know that you go out and do classes by yourself. Remember to be the person you want your child to be.

Learn the Steps

This book is about the 5 steps to confidence that will rub off on your child; so remember, when you take these actions, you're not only doing them for yourself, but you're doing them for the good of your family, and mainly your children. You want your child to be the best that they can be, and for them to be like that, they need to have confidence within themselves. In my opinion, the best way for a child to have confidence is to have a confident parent, guiding them along their journey and showing them the best way to go. You cannot force children to do anything and, in my opinion, nor should we. Our children are blessings and should be appreciated as so. I have known a lot of parents who guide their children according to their own beliefs and past regrets. This is very sad because it is not the child's fault that you never got to fulfil your life the way you wanted to. You probably all know a mum who heavily influences their daughter to go to ballet, just because she always wanted to go when she was a young child but never got the chance. Your child was born with their own unique abilities and talents, and you should allow these abilities and talents to flow freely from your child anyway that they choose to. Allow them to try activities and classes, but do not force your own desires onto them—let them experiment with what feels good to them.

The Motivated Mummies' Guide to Confidence

"Everyone needs a coach. It doesn't matter whether you're a basketball player, a tennis player, a gymnast, or a bridge player."
– Bill Gates

One of the most important things I think we can install in our children is to be teachable. To have an open mind and be open to learning is so very valuable at any age. I held a workshop last week on Tony Robbins' 6 human needs, at a charity event. One man approached the workshop and asked what it was about. When I mentioned that it was Tony Robbins' strategies, he said he didn't like him, and he turned around and walked out. This was a slight blow to my confidence, as I had never met anybody that disliked Tony Robbins before, and I had been confident of my content. But remembering just how much he had changed my life, I said to the man, "That's okay; we all have our opinions," and I smiled. He then turned around and said, "Do you know what? I promised myself I would be… (I can't repeat what he said because it was rude; but basically, he said that he would be more open minded this year, so he would come in, and he would listen!) No pressure on me then! But I was glad he changed his mind, and I was glad to hear that his New Year's resolution was to be more open-minded.

I am thankful to tell you that at the end of the workshop, he approached me, took my hand, and said, "Thank you very much," and that he had indeed learnt something positive. He said he was glad that he had stayed and listened. I think I was even gladder that he had stayed and listened, because I know me, and I would have carried that with me to the next event, maybe not being as confident in holding a workshop on the 6 human needs again.

Partaking in the free event boosted my confidence and my ability in public speaking. I became one step closer to my dreams and goals, and as I've just explained, there were hurdles along the way. It wasn't all smooth sailing, but it was worth doing. This gentleman was in his 60s, I'm guessing, as he said he was retired. Just imagine how different his life could have been if he had taken the attitude of being more teachable from a young age? What would he have learnt by sticking around and listening to others just that little bit more often?

How teachable are you? Do you listen to other people's opinions? Are you open to learning and to new knowledge? Are you teaching your children to be open to learning new facts and new perspectives on life?

We can all learn. It does not matter how intellectual we are or how much or how little studying we have done previously; at any age, at any point, we can always learn more. I have heard many people say that they do not have time to study or time to learn. I'm just going to call it how I see it, and say that is crap. We all have 24 hours in a day, and when you have people like Richard Branson running numerous businesses and continuing to educate themselves and grow, I will not hear the excuse that you didn't have time. I hear you saying that it's OK for him because he's a man, and he doesn't have to do the cooking and the cleaning, as well as running businesses and looking after the children—of course, he has time! I follow a lady called Dani Johnson, and she will blow any of your excuses out of the water—she did mine! She is a mother of 5, and she was homeless at 19, and a multi-millionaire by 21, running numerous businesses and dedicating a huge amount of time and money to charity.

She often does YouTube clips, demonstrating how she cooks up big batches of food to feed all her family, and her tips on saving money are great. Her ideas on structuring your day so that you get everything done is just fantastic. Just because you can multitask, it doesn't mean you should. One of my favourite quotes by Dani is:

"Pray with your feet."

Dani is a very religious person, unlike myself, but I still use this quote often. She says that yes, you should ask for what you want, and pray, but you must also take action, because without action, you will never achieve your true goals.

Whether you are religious or not, I highly recommend you look up Dani Johnson on YouTube, or invest in one of her books or CDs. She is such a fabulous role model for a busy working mum. I have used many of her tips and strategies in my coaching and workshops, as I find them highly effective.

Back to the no excuses, how could you learn more without taking up any extra time? As I have just said, people like Dani Johnson often have CDs, which are great for listening to in the car instead of the radio, and these will be fantastic for helping your children to learn more as they have no escape while they're in the car. It may be background noise, but it will be sinking into the subconscious. Another great tip is YouTube. We are so fortunate to have so much free information at our fingertips! I often play a YouTube clip as I'm getting ready in the morning, doing my hair and makeup, and I also play these while I'm cooking dinner. Most people have smartphones these days, where you can download audio books, podcasts, and probably many other things that I'm not techy enough to tell you about, but I do know there are many ways to listen to information, and you can do this while you're doing something else that doesn't need concentration.

It amazes me when people turn around and say they don't have time, but then, in the next sentence, they asked me if I saw EastEnders last night. I'm not saying that anybody that watches television is bad, but does that mean you're sitting down at 7:30pm and then just watching telly for 4 hours? Could you possibly prioritise half an hour during the evening to feed your mind with something more positive than the negative drama of a soap from the telly? Maybe, if you walk the dog, you could listen to an audiobook while you're walking. I sometimes listen to the audio book, Ask the Universe, while I'm walking George, my Greyhound. It's something that can easily be listened to without having to concentrate too much. When I'm at the gym, I put on my headphones, and I listen to the music from the UPW seminar, or a Tony Robbins speech. This fills me with positive affirmations, and it is so much better than watching the subtitles of the depressing news, on the telly, in the gym.

There are many little snippets of time that you could use to feed your brain. You do not have to give up hours and sit with a pen and paper and study what you're listening to. It will all sink in slowly.

Lots of people ask me who I listen to. My list is long, but I personally believe that you will find the right person for you at the right time of your life. I have friends that swear by certain people, but I just can't get to grips with them at the moment, so my suggestion would be to go on the internet, whether that be YouTube or another platform, and search motivational speakers. See who you resonate with, and that will probably be who you need to listen to at this moment in time. Following on from that, once you have found your ideal people to be your role model, you could always look them up on Facebook or social media platforms, and join groups that follow them. This way, you will also meet new people who again have the same interests as you.

ACTION

- What do you need to learn/do to gain confidence in each area written in Chapter 2?
- What may stop you from doing this?
* If that happens, how can you combat that so you don't fail?

Notes

Chapter 4

Be Yourself – Everyone Else Is Taken

Step 3: Accept Who You Are

The first step to increasing your confidence is to accept who you are. For some people, that is a lot easier said than done, but once we can truly accept ourselves, it allows us the freedom to grow and build from where we are. Acceptance does not mean seeing your limitations and not doing anything about them. Acceptance is understanding and appreciating who you are now, which will then enable you, if you so choose, to grow and develop in the areas that you feel you are not as strong. Many people have a strong feeling that they are not good enough, and this has devastating effects on your confidence. This feeling can develop from a major incident in your life or a run of small, less easy to identify events.

> *"However, my parents, both of whom came from impoverished backgrounds and neither of whom had been to college, took the view that my overactive imagination was an amusing quirk that would never pay a mortgage or secure a pension."*
> *– J. K. Rowling*

I will be speaking to you more on growing and developing, in the next chapter of the book, but for now, we need to understand the importance of accepting who we are right now.

The Motivated Mummies' Guide to Confidence

"Be yourself as everyone else is taken."
– Oscar Wilde

I love that quote, and it's so true; we often watch people and wish we could be like them. Realising that we are who we are, and because of that we are so very special, is a very liberating feeling. For years, I felt that I was not good enough, and that it was only me that had this feeling. I now realise that you probably have this feeling too, as it is extremely common. Tony Robbins often says that there are two fears in this world: the fear of not being loved, and the fear of not being good enough.

In this day and age, we are often comparing ourselves to others. With the overuse of social media, we compare our lives to the ones we see plastered on our phones and laptops. Limiting your use of such forms of entertainment is a vital way of improving your mental well-being, especially at times when you are not feeling your best. When you are highly motivated, and feeling like you can conquer the world, you love to see others doing well, but if you are having a down day, or are feeling a little stuck, then the last thing you want to see is how well everyone else is doing.

You may have many positive groups, and follow many positive leaders on Facebook, Instagram, and Twitter, but it will still enforce the underlying feeling of not being good enough. When we see others being highly motivated and driven, and we are not feeling it ourselves, and when we see others fulfilling their dreams, and we feel we are not fulfilling ours, it will not help build our confidence. Although it is much better to follow these positive people, I would still suggest rationing your use of such media to just a couple of minutes a day, if you cannot go without it completely.

Take a few minutes to look at your social media. Who are you following? Whose beliefs and ideas of how the world should be are you surrounding yourself with? Thoughts and ideas are being drip fed to us every second of every day. Look at the adverts you see on the telly, the train, sides of buses, and on the programmes you watch. These are all what society thinks you should be seeing. Society is not always right. Society does not have your well-being at heart; society is generally out to sell you something that they want you to buy into. I know that sounds very cynical, but if you don't stop and smell the roses occasionally, then it is very easy to be swept along and be one of the crowd. And although there's comfort in numbers, you do not want to be in that crowd.

Did you know that most people are not happy, and that most people are not satisfied in some way or another? Do you really want to be one of the crowd, or would you like to be different? Different is good; different is what you were born to be. If we were all meant to look the same and have the same thoughts and ideas, we would have all be born identical. Imagine that!

You may not be in control of the adverts you are surrounded by, but you are 100% in control of the books you read, the apps you download, and the people you choose to follow. Just make sure they have your best interests at heart. As a coach, I am fully aware of the power of selling your life on social media. I have been told to do it myself. It's a kind of *"look at me, look how happy I am, would you like to be as happy as me?"* thing; and yes, I have been sucked in to it too! I have been told to only post pictures of myself looking great, so that the world sees me as altogether, but as The Motivated Mummies Transformation Group is all about accepting who you are and having confidence in yourself, I never put a filter on my face (unless I'm posting a picture my kids have taken with me, and I have silly reindeer ears or something obvious like that). My pictures are of me, wrinkles and all, sometimes with makeup, sometimes without, sometimes looking and feeling good, sometimes not! I try hard to post a variety of posts that are accurate to my life, and not edited to only portray happiness. No one is happy 24/7; with all the good intentions in the world, crap still happens, and we are all human. I am a coach, and I have learnt how to overcome problems quickly, not eliminate them completely—no one can do that.

I have grown so confident over the last couple of years that I am okay with what I look like (which is different than thinking I look damn hot all the time), and I often do my live videos straight from the gym—no makeup, hair a mess, and thank God, it's not smell vision! Occasionally, I will apologise for the state of myself, but really, that is just out of habit. You can't go from thinking you need to look your best all the time to not caring at the snap of a finger; it takes time to adjust to your new thoughts and feelings.

> *"It's not all bad. Heightened self-consciousness, apartness, an inability to join in, physical shame and self-loathing—they are not all bad. Those devils have been my angels. Without them, I would never have disappeared into language, literature, the mind, laughter, and all the mad intensities that made and unmade me."*
> – Stephen Fry

I remember when I was about 17 years old, maybe older, and I needed to go to a local shop. As I have said, I had social phobia, and this made leaving the house very difficult some days. Today was one of those days. I mustered up the courage and walked to the shops I needed. It was about a 12- minute walk. I got there, bought 2 of the 5 things I needed, and couldn't cope any longer. I just felt so ugly that I shouldn't, and couldn't, be out any longer! I grabbed my things and literally ran all the way home until I was safe behind my closed door again. There is no rational thinking when you have a fear, and my fear was being out of my house, because I didn't have confidence in myself. I didn't have enough confidence in my appearance to go buy a few items from the shop! How sad is that? It just shows the importance of confidence and self-esteem. It must have been traumatic for it to stick in my head for all these years, yet now I look back and think, what the hell? What on earth was I bothered about? But if your mental health is not in a good place, then these are the issues you face every single day!

> "Success? I don't know what that word means. I'm happy. But success, that goes back to what in somebody's eyes success means. For me, success is inner peace. That's a good day for me."
> – Denzel Washington

It's because I faced these that I am determined to help others feel better about themselves. Life is too short to feel ugly. After all, who says what is ugly and what is pretty? Beauty is in the eye of the beholder. We all find different people physically attractive, yet the adverts and the telly programmes (society) say that it has to be A, B & C. I am here to say that it doesn't! X Y & Z can be damn hot too! True beauty comes from within. If you are a kind-hearted person, and you allow yourself to be confident, that is really very attractive. So, stop comparing yourself to others, throw back your shoulders, and put on some confidence. Wear it like an outfit until it slowly sinks in and becomes your second skin.

> "Setting goals is the first step in turning the invisible into the visible."
> – Tony Robbins

Whose Eyes Does She Have?

It is no wonder we struggle to accept ourselves as individuals, when from the moment we are born, the biggest question is who we look like. We often crave to fit in and to be one of the crowd, but we are not all born that way. Each one of you has a unique and special gift or talent, which, when nurtured and allowed to grow, helps you to turn into a unique and beautiful person. Acknowledging the fact that you are special and one-of-a-kind can be very liberating, and can relieve some of the pressure of conforming.

We are who we are. Each and every one of us was born unique. Some of you might look like your brothers, sisters, mum or dad, but you all have your own unique and special ways. You have talents and gifts that are just yours, and a special feature that is completely your own identity. We are who we are, warts and all. It is sometimes hard to accept who we are, and there are many different reasons for this. I had a client who struggled to feel beautiful. As we spoke and went deep into the conversation, it came out that her mother was always putting herself down. She would always comment that she was too fat or too short, or her nose was too crocked, or her hair too wiry and her eyes too squinty. She has done this ever since my client could remember; so, from a young age, my client's role model was a woman that was not happy with the way she looked. Although her mother often told her that she was pretty, she would also hear from other people that she was the spitting image of her mum. This left my client confused. How could she be pretty, if her own mother was telling her that she wasn't—not directly, of course; she would never do that. It was no wonder my client was confused. If she was the spitting image of her mum, and her mum was ugly, in her eyes, it must mean that she, herself, was ugly—after all, you believe what your mum tells you. We all have times of low confidence, and as mums, our bodies have changed so dramatically after giving birth that it can take some time to get used to our new shapes. Some women never get over the loss of their pre-baby body, and mourn this for many years. Personally, I believe that just because you have had a baby doesn't mean you cannot have a banging body again; it just takes a little more effort and a tub of skin tightening cream!

A belief is something that we tell ourselves over and over again until it is ingrained in us. My client's mother told herself over and over that she was ugly, to the point that she believed it, and then to the point that my client started to believe that she was ugly too. No amount of wishful thinking can make you change how you look, and no amount of regret or remorse for who you are can change anything. There are obviously things you can do to improve your looks, but the best thing you can do is to accept who you are and work on your confidence. Confidence and a smile can instantly make you more attractive to everyone that sees you. Yes, you can *fake it till you make it*. We will learn more on this, later in the book.

Learn How You Tick

Self-development is a great way to develop acceptance, and to learn who you truly are. It is not until you investigate yourself deeply that you can understand yourself more, and how you tick. When I studied the Core 100 coaching programme by Tony Robbins, I actively decided with each module that I would use the skills and strategies on myself before applying them to anybody else. It is very easy to read or learn something, and think how it will help someone else, but it is not so easy to think how it can apply to yourself, and then put it into action to see the results. I knew, if I wanted to be a good, successful life coach, I would need to ensure that I used the strategies that I was going to preach to others. You cannot tell somebody to do something that you haven't done yourself first. I see this with many coaches and therapists. It is hard to hold that mirror up sometimes, but by having a coach myself, I ensure that I am always learning, growing, and assessing myself too.

Learning the six human needs was one of the most important things I have ever learnt in my whole 39 years. It made everything fall into place, and it makes complete sense. It not only helped me to gain understanding of my own actions, but also the actions of others around me. Each one of you reacts and acts in a certain way because of your top human need. This information alone is truly life changing. When I discovered that my top need at the time was certainty, it shone a light on all the decisions that I had made over many years. My crippling anxiety had all been based around my need for certainty, which was so strong. I craved control, routine, and security in my life, and in the life of the people that I loved. At any point when I felt I was not in control, I would literally go into panic mode, and as you cannot be in control of everybody all the time, it was no wonder that I spent my life feeling anxious and stressed.

I speak more on this in The Motivated Mummies transformation group, so for now, let's concentrate on building your confidence. So, what is your top need? Could it be certainty as well? Or maybe it's variety, significance, or love and connection. Or are you further down the road of self-help, and maybe it is growth or contribution? Our top need changes as we develop as people. Now that I have grown and learnt new techniques and strategies, my top need has moved from certainty, to growth and contribution. This takes a huge amount of pressure off my shoulders, and has allowed me to live a more relaxed lifestyle. Learning this information on the 6 human needs, and my Tony Robbins coaching course, has given me a huge amount of confidence in my everyday life. You can find more information on Tony Robbins and his teachings and upcoming seminars, on my book website: www.themotivatedmummiesguidetoconfidence.com.

The first step to increasing your confidence is to accept who you are. For some people, that is a lot easier said than done, but once you can truly accept yourself, it allows you the freedom to grow and build from where you are. Acceptance does not mean seeing your limitations and not doing anything about them. Acceptance is understanding and appreciating who you are, which will then enable you, if you so choose, to grow and develop in the areas that you feel you are not as strong. Acknowledging the fact that you are special, unique, and one-of-a-kind can be very liberating, and can relieve some of the pressure of conforming. Seeing this growth in my clients, and helping them to develop and become happier, is such a thrill, and one of the reasons I love my job!

Within coaching, I work on a lot of core beliefs. We all have a set of core beliefs, which we have picked up along the way. You have these around your own abilities, and even around your confidence. Deep down, you have attachments to those beliefs, and that is why you live your life as you do. When working with a coach, they will challenge your beliefs if they feel they are *limiting*, which means they are doing you no good by believing them. They will reframe situations and ask you to look at life from a different angle, all in aid of changing those limiting beliefs to ones that can help you along in life. You may not even realise you have these beliefs that need working on, but a trained coach will spot them a mile off, and help you to nip them in the bud so you can move on.

Most beliefs come from your upbringing, and any negative ones are not done on purpose, but these harming beliefs can be picked up anywhere as your life goes along, so it's important to check in with someone every now and then to shake them off—a detox for the soul, if you like. Another great way to help build positive beliefs is to surround yourself with great role models. These can be people you admire from afar, like celebrities and experts in their field, or friends that you admire and look up to.

"You're the average of the five people you spend the most time with." – Jim Rohn

Forgive and Heal

Forgiveness is a huge part of accepting who you are. We are all formed from the trials and tribulations that we have been through. Each event, whether it is good or bad, helps to form the person that we become. By accepting who we are, and learning to love ourselves, we can then forgive anyone who we previously thought had done us wrong. If it had not been for these people and those situations, we would not be the strong, determined people that we are now. So, if anything, we should be grateful for the hardships we have been through, and for the pain that we have been put through, because without those, we would not have learnt and grown.

Society would have you think that you are doing the right thing to hold onto your bitterness—why should you forgive those who have done you wrong, especially in extreme cases? Following the masses is never a good idea though. Most people are not happy and fulfilled; very few have truly found inner peace. Inner peace does not come from following society or the masses; it comes from believing in your heart what you know is true, and having the courage to follow that.

My dad left when I was nearly 11 years old. He left all five children, didn't pay for their upbringing, and stopped sending cards or birthday presents. I had gone from being a daddy's girl to being nothing—not important, not loved, and not wanted. I was quite in my right to be angry and upset, and to not forgive him. I held on to this anger and pain for over 25 years, and 25 years is a very long time to hold on to so much pain, but I didn't realise there was an alternative option. Both society and my family believed he was not to be forgiven. Why should he be? After everything he'd done, he did not deserve it. That is very true; he did not deserve to be forgiven—but I did. I deserved to be able to let go of the pain and suffering that I was going through by holding on to my anger for him. I did deserve to have the best life I could have, and not let his poor decision-making ruin my life forever—I did deserve that.

It was not until I went to Tony Robbins' UPW seminar in London, on April 2017, that I realised this. He says that if you are not happy with your life, or an area in it, look for a new role model for that area. This does not mean leaving your important people behind, but accepting them for who they are, taking their good bits on board, and choosing to follow somebody else's way of living for other bits. I love my family dearly, and they give me a huge amount of support and comfort, but for this aspect of my life, they were not a good role model. I needed to follow a different way of thinking in order to be happy. You can have as many role models as you like; in fact, you should have many role models in all different areas of your life. Seek out someone who has what you want, and copy them, because they have already figured it out.

"I have not failed. I've just found 10,000 ways that won't work."
– Thomas Edison

At the seminar, Tony spoke of the 6 human needs, and explained why people make the decisions that they do. I had often been told by my friends and therapists that it was not my fault that my dad had left. I never thought for a second that it was my fault; I just believed that if I had done something differently, he would still want to be around me. It was my belief that if I had been more lovable, he would not have stopped seeing me.

Tony helped us realise that people act according to their top human need, and through the four days that I was there participating in UPW, I learnt that my dad had acted on his top need, and was purely doing the best he could do for himself. Even if he did love me, his top need was significance and love and connection, and as a teenager going through a stressful situation, I couldn't give him either of those. I was able, for the first time in my life, to step back and look in at the situation. This made it much easier to see that it really was nothing to do with me, and all to do with him and his needs. As human beings, we are not born knowing the answers; we can only rely on what we have learnt growing up, and from the environment around us.

I have learnt that I am a caring and loving person, and I will often think of others before myself, but that is because of the way I have been raised, and the situations I have faced on my journey. If I had not gone through the pain and suffering that I had, I would not necessarily be like that, so we have to forgive others who do not have the same beliefs and values as ourselves. People are purely doing what they know best, and that is not necessarily going to be the same as what you know to be best. By finally being able to forgive my dad for his actions, it enabled me to let go of the pain and suffering that I was going through. You do not have to forgive people for their benefit, but you do have to forgive them for your own. Who could you forgive today that would make your life better?

"It's what you learn after you know it all that counts."
– John Wooden

Talk to Yourself Nicely

Once you have learnt to accept yourself and others, you must start talking to yourself as your new best friend. Your words and inner voice are of utmost importance to your confidence; you can either knock yourself down or build yourself up—it's your choice. A belief is something that you have been told often—so often that it is ingrained to your core. It makes sense then that if every day you are talking negatively to yourself, you will inevitably feel less important. If you make the effort to speak to yourself in a supportive, positive way, you will, over time, believe that you are worth speaking to like that. Others will speak to you more respectfully too, because you will not put up with anything less.

You may not even realise to start with that you're talking to yourself in a negative tone; you may be so used to hearing it that you have not yet identified that it's a problem. If you are unaware if your inner voice is positive or negative, I suggest your first starting point would be to listen to what you are saying to yourself. Make a point, throughout the day, to focus on your inner voice and the kind of things it is saying to you. As we said in step 1, the first task is to identify the problem. Identify your language to yourself, and then take step 2, which is to learn from what you have discovered. Is your inner voice helpful or detrimental to your happiness and your confidence? Knowledge is power. Use the knowledge, accept your inner voice, and then take action to improve it.

> "Everyone has that inner voice, the one that's a Negative Nancy. I'd say to ignore that voice and to be confident and follow your heart."
> – Katharine McPhee

Set yourself a challenge to praise yourself every day. Acknowledge at least two or three things that you like about yourself and congratulate yourself on something that you have achieved that day. This action alone will start the wheels turning to build your confidence and is a fantastic activity to do with your children. Before they go to bed, ask them what their *wins* were for today. What did they do that they were pleased with? What did they do today to make themselves proud? It is extremely important to encourage them to be proud of themselves. Quite often, we live for the recognition of our parents, and for them to be proud of us, but they will not be around forever, and once they have gone, it can leave a gaping hole that can never be filled. When teaching your child to be proud of themselves, they will not be left with such a gaping hole once you are not around.

It is also important for you to tell your child what you have done that day that has made you proud of yourself. Remember that you are the role model for them, and they are copying your behaviour, not what you tell them to do. If you sit with them every night and ask them about their achievements, and tell them about yours, it is not only a bonding time for you both, but they will see that you are living a fulfilled and happy life, and that is what they should do too. It is habits like these that get taught and handed down; so the chances are, they will sit with their children and talk about their successes too (great to know you started that!). These are all very positive activities that are vital in achieving ultimate success. Be the person you want your child to be.

ACTION

* Write a list of all your good points. You can ask friends and family to add to the list. This is a great activity to do with the whole family, and to improve your children's self-esteem too.
• What are you proud of today? Start asking yourself this every day, and discuss with your child.

Notes

Chapter 5

Practice What You Preach

Step 4: Take Action

> *"Change will not come if we wait for some other person or some other time. We are the ones we've been waiting for. We are the change that we seek."*
> – Barack Obama

Step 4 is, in my opinion, the most important step of the five steps. If you do not take action, then it doesn't matter how much you read. If you are not putting it into practice, it is pointless learning it. This step is the difference between people who succeed and people who do not. It is said that only 2% of the population are successful, because they do not only think about things; they follow them through. If you have done any of the steps so far, and are taking any of the actions in the action plans, then I give you my heartfelt congratulations, because you are in the minority, and you are freaking awesome! You and your determination and attitude toward life will be demonstrating to your child a fantastic role model. It may not seem very important to fill out notes in a book, but if you are taking action to write in the book, what else are you taking action to do? The same goes for the other way around. If you cannot even pick up a pencil to write in a book, where else are you not taking action in life? If you are in that 2%, that's fantastic. For the rest of the 98 percenters, stop reading, go grab a pencil, and fill out a question. You can break the habit at any point in life, so break it right now by filling out the action step in a previous chapter.

> *"The path to success is to take massive, determined action."*
> –Tony Robbins

For any of you who do not complete any of the work in the book, I need you to take a closer look at what are you gaining from this behaviour. Every behaviour has a good intention, but it may not have the perfect outcome. If there is something in life that you know you should do, and you're just not doing it, stop and think why you are not doing it—what is the intention behind that? It is usually some sort of protection system. If you have not yet managed to take action throughout reading this book, take a minute to think why that could be. You may not be aware of it, but deep down you may want to stay lacking in confidence because, in some way, shape, or form, it is benefiting you. This might sound crazy, but when you look at it at a deeper level, you will realise that you are getting at least one of your 6 human needs met by staying unconfident.

As I have said before, it is much easier to work these things out in a one-to-one coaching session, as it is easier for a trained coach to pick up on the deeper reasons of why you do things. Having trained with Tony Robbins, and learnt the six human needs inside and out, I find it quite easy to spot the different vehicles of meeting your needs. I also feel confident in telling you that negative actions fulfil our needs. Having lived with anxiety and depression, I am now fully able to look back and realise that my needs were being completely met by that negative route. It takes a strong person to accept that their negative behaviour is benefiting them, but once you are able to do that, it frees you up to living a happier and more fulfilled life.

> *"Only put off until tomorrow what you are willing to die having left undone."*
> – Pablo Picasso

What Does Taking Action Look Like?

The sheer process of putting one foot in front of the other, and doing what you know you should be doing, is empowering, and gives you a sense of achievement. Doing an action once is beneficial, but doing it repeatedly will bring significant results that could change your life forever. Doing something once can be empowering, but when you take that action and repeat it, you gain confidence in your ability, and you get better and better. Even if the action is uncomfortable to start with, or you may not enjoy it, if you do it often, it becomes routine and will eventually meet your need for certainty (however uncertain it feels to start with). This is why it is becoming so popular to have a coach, because a coach will hold you accountable for your actions, and will ensure that you do take the action that you're supposed to be taking, again and again, until it becomes more comfortable for you. There are many ways that coaches work, but they often like to book you in for more than one session, preferably more than 1 month at a time, because they understand the importance of momentum. If you go to see a coach and have a one-off session, you will get some changes, and you will see some progress, but if you booked in for 6 months to a year, with a life coach, you will see momentous achievements, huge progress, and amazing success! This is because momentum has taken place, and you are building block after block on top of your foundation. Imagine a house being built: You lay down your foundation in your first session; then, the next time you go back to your coach, you build the next layer of blocks; and then the next time you go back, you build the next layer. If you only went back to see your coach two or three times, you would have a little wall; whereas if you went back every week for 6 months, you could build your dream house! This is how coaching works. It is not a scam to get more money out of you; it is because we understand the importance of momentum and the huge benefits of taking consistent action.

"Do one thing every day that scares you."
– Eleanor Roosevelt

Some people just have an accountability coach. This is where the coach holds the client accountable for their actions. In the session, a client will say what they would like to achieve, and a coach will check in and firmly but nicely ensure that the client has successfully completed each task that they wanted to get done. The coach would then be able to help the client if there was anything blocking them from doing those tasks. Sometimes, in life, all we need is to know that somebody will be checking that we've done it, and that's enough to get our butt moving.

"Keep your face to the sunshine and you cannot see a shadow."
– Helen Keller

Compliment Someone Daily

We spoke earlier about learning to accept yourself, and about the importance of a positive inner voice. Now we are going to address the importance of an outer voice. Often, in life, we have thoughts about other people and their actions, which can be negative or positive, and for the most part, we keep these thoughts to ourselves. From now on, if you have a positive thought about a person, and they are standing in front of you, I would like you to speak that thought to them. For example, if you are paying a cashier, and she has a particularly nice lipstick on, just say, "I really like the colour of your lipstick." This small action has two big benefits: One, it will probably make her day to be complimented; and two, it will boost your confidence. Believe it or not, it takes confidence to give a compliment.

You may have an inner voice telling you not to do it: "What if she laughs at me? What if she thinks I'm weird for saying it? What if she does not accept the compliment?" What if? Does it really matter? The chances of her not accepting the compliment, and brushing it off, are quite high; not many people are good at accepting compliments—that takes practice too. But I guarantee, whether she smiles and says thank you, or she brushes it off, it will still boost her confidence, and the next time she goes to put her makeup on, she will more likely choose that lip colour, knowing that somebody else likes it, which will give her that little bit of extra confidence. So, by building confidence yourself, you can give it to others at the same time. How good does that feel? This technique is simple, but it does take practice. The first few times you want to do it, you may not go through with it, but keep persevering. There will be a time when you feel more comfortable to give out the compliment, and if you keep practicing, it will become easier and easier. You will also find that if you give honest compliments, you will have more friends, and people will warm to you more. People can see through false compliments, and that will not go over well, so only do it when you really feel it, and you will be surprised at the outcome.

Eliminate Negative Energy Drainers

As you read this, you are likely to have a variety of personalities in your life: Some will be high energy and fun, while others will be lower energy or negative; some will be proactive, while others will be reactive. There is a famous saying: *You can't choose your family, but you can choose your friends.* This is very true, and it's very important which friends you do choose. I am not going to tell you to drop all your friends who have problems, and to surround yourself with positive people only, as that is not realistic; but I will tell you to be careful of who you spend the majority of your time with. Have you heard of the concept that you are the five people closest to you? Take a minute to think who the five people are that you are closest to. Are they positive, proactive, supportive, healthy, and fulfilled?

If you put one person in a group of 5, and the group are all of the above, you will be lifted to their beliefs and their values, and you will become like them. On the other hand, if you put one person in a group of 5, and they are negative, unhealthy, and reactive, you will ultimately become like them. For this reason, it is very important to acknowledge who you spend the majority of your time with. If you know that you are going to merge into them, you may choose differently. If you are in a position at the moment, where most of your friends are in the latter category, I suggest you broaden your social activities in search of some new friends. This does not mean you have to drop your old friends; you just reduce the amount of time you spend with them. The same goes with your family. If they are dragging you down all the time, instead of lifting you up, limit your time with them. You can love them from afar, be supportive toward them, and help lift them up, but do not get dragged down by them. This may sound unkind, but if you surround yourself with positive people and get lifted up by them, you are much more able to go and lift up your friends and family who are not yet as happy as you. You can see this activity as helping your friends and family, and not as dropping them like a hot potato. Once your friends and family see the improvement in your life and your attitude, they will want it for themselves, and they too may go out and seek a more beneficial friendship group. You could be the start of a positive chain reaction for everyone you know and love.

"Once you replace negative thoughts with positive ones, you'll start having positive results."
– Willie Nelson

The Power of Momentum

In the world of coaching and accomplishments, momentum is of utmost importance. I have worked with many clients, and those who book courses with the intention of working on a goal, see a much greater success rate than those who book in sporadically. When you work on something consistently, it not only becomes easier, but it becomes more natural, so as you go through this book and look at the techniques and strategies that you need to put in place, I urge you to do something toward your confidence each and every day. It does not matter the size of your effort, just that the momentum is kept up. Momentum is much more important than the action you take.

Practice What You Preach

"Success is the sum of small efforts, repeated day in and day out."
– Robert Collier

I started going to the gym a few years back, and at the beginning it was extremely hard to get my butt out the door and down the road to the gym, and it was only 5 minutes away from my home. The effort was huge, and some days—actually most days—I did not want to go. On the days that I really felt like giving in, I told myself to just go for the momentum. I went with the intention to go for 10 minutes and do some stretches. I did not want to get to the point where I had to start again. As you know, starting anything is the hardest part. Some days, I would go with the intention of going for 10 minutes, and end up staying 30 minutes, and in my eyes, that was a win, because at least I had gotten there.

Take this attitude with you on your journey to confidence, and if you can, take big actions, because you will get big results. If you cannot, take small actions, and just keep the momentum going. The aim is to never have to start again. Momentum is one of the major benefits of having a coach. You are booked in weekly, fortnightly, or monthly, but you know that those sessions will happen, and you know there will be consistent improvement in your life. Each coaching session builds on the last, and it is like a snowball effect, rolling along the ground, getting bigger, and bigger, and bigger, and your results get bigger, and bigger, and bigger, and your life gets better, and better, and better! You can achieve goals by yourself—of course, you can—but it is just much faster to work alongside a coach. You will be pushed quite often outside of your comfort zone, because that is where you grow and learn the most.

"The difference between winning and losing
is most often not quitting."
– Walt Disney

I spoke earlier about the 6 human needs being vital to understand, with most people craving certainty above all else. Starting a new activity is sometimes scary, and your brain will try and fight it, as it is designed to protect you from anything unknown, in case it kills you. Let your heart rule the way, and persevere, because it will soon become natural, and anything you do often enough becomes a habit, which equals certainty and safety again.

> *"People have a need for certainty, and that need for certainty is in every human being—certainty that you can avoid pain, certainty that you can at least be comfortable. It's a survival instinct."*
> – Tony Robbins

Regardless if you have a coach or not, set yourself challenges on a regular basis. If you can join up with others, this is much better, as you can hold each other accountable for your actions, and this alone is enough to push some people forward. Ensure that these challenges are achievable; they should be a little out of your comfort zone, but they must fit into your everyday life in order for you to attempt them. If you plan something too intricate, which takes too much time and effort, you will have a perfect excuse not to do it; whereas by planning something simple that fits in with the flow of your day, you have no excuses, and it's easier to achieve. As I said before, being aware of who you associate with is important, and one easy way to surround yourself with more proactive people is to join an accountability group. Sometimes you are not able to be in close contact with who you want to be surrounded by, but you can still have access to their beliefs and values. You could always start your own WhatsApp group, and encourage others to post both their struggles and their wins, and then support each other. Supporting and encouraging other people also helps to build your confidence and your sense of fulfilment in life. Do not ever believe that you need to be perfect before you can help other people; you only need to be one step ahead of them to be able to help them forward. It is important to allow them to help you too, as this gives them a sense of achievement, and also helps improve the trust between the two of you. Life is all about flow; what comes in, must go out, in order to keep the flow moving happily. If you would like to find out how I can help you move forward in your life, and achieve your goals quicker, visit my website: www.motivatedmummies.com.

Belief Turns to Action

You've read the book, and you know what to do—but why do it? Why take action? Action is the part that will improve your life; self-help is just shelf-help, if you only read the books. Taking action and doing what you read is what will make those changes. Look at the chart below. You have tons of potential (as do your children), and by doing something outside your comfort zone, you learn. You may not do it correctly or as good as you hoped, but you will learn from it, and you will be better than before. You WILL see results. By seeing these results, you will realise you have potential to do more. You take more ACTION, and you see more RESULTS, and this makes your BELIEF go up. If you take MASSIVE ACTION, you will see MASSIVE RESULTS, and you will feel MASSIVE BELIEF in yourself. This cycle continues, and you will feel UNSTOPPABLE! Now, imagine teaching that to your children; imagine the lives they could have if they saw that their mum was UNSTOPPABLE! They would know they were UNSTOPPABLE too!

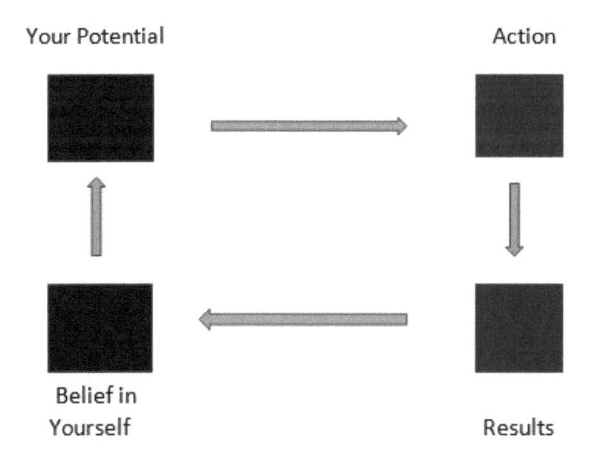

For many people lacking in confidence, the thought of doing anything out of their comfort zone is terrifying. If you have read those words and felt sick to your stomach, yet continue to read, then well done—you are obviously a fighter! Everybody has a comfort zone, although some people's comfort zones are larger than others, but it is always possible to step out and grow. The thing about taking action is that it increases the size of your comfort zone; so the more action you take, the bigger surface area you have in which to feel comfortable. When I got my life back, I described it as feeling free. I literally felt like I could do anything, and I was not trapped anymore. Sometimes our comfort zones get very claustrophobic if they are not stretched. I still work on my own confidence on a daily basis. I have never said I am the most confident person in the world. This book is all about building your confidence, from nothing to a quiet, content confidence. I have an underlying confidence in myself now, but of course, like everybody, I have areas that I need to improve. I still take the advice that I am giving you, and I work daily on building my confidence in areas that it is lacking. I used to be afraid to speak to people, as I had no confidence, so I took my own advice. I first identified the problem of public speaking, and then I found the knowledge that I needed at Toastmasters, and experts in public speaking. I then accepted who I was, and my own abilities, and finally, I took action. Because of this, I was recently able to speak in front of 80 people at my wedding. There would have been no way I could have done this without following the steps first. I had so many people congratulate me on my achievement and my wedding speech, and I felt very proud of myself for being able to do it.

> *"The first step toward success is taken when you refuse to be a captive of the environment in which you first find yourself."*
> – Mark Caine

The most important strategy I learnt to help conquer my fears was a three-step process. When you start to take action to build your confidence, you are bound to feel nervous and afraid; so, learning this

Practice What You Preach

three-step strategy will help you to achieve your goals and build your confidence. When a situation occurs, you must mentally step back and assess yourself. Ask yourself three very important questions: 1. What am I focused on? 2. What is my body doing right now? 3. What is my inner voice telling me? These three questions will help you to conquer any situation. If you are feeling nervous, you will be focused on something detrimental, your body language will be guarded or tense, and your inner voice will no doubt be telling you something negative. By asking yourself these 3 questions, you can adjust yourself to the situation, and progress in a much more proactive manner. For example, imagine if you are at work, and your boss has asked you to brief the room about the ongoing project. Your initial feeling could be panic! Your focus may be on what you will say wrong; your body language could be extremely tense (and you could be a little sweaty now), and your inner voice will be saying very unhelpful things, like "Oh, my goodness, I can't do this. Why did he pick me? I'm not good enough to stand up and talk in front of everybody."

When you get the feeling of panic, that is when you need to ask the three questions. Let's call them the Panic Rules. Question 1: What are you focused on? If you are focused on what you will say wrong, this will not help you in the situation, so change your focus to something completely different. This could be how pretty your teammate's dress is today, how you're going to treat yourself to your favourite coffee once you finish this talk, or how you can help your colleagues create their best project yet! The more powerful the focus, the better. If your focus is on helping people, it takes the pressure away from yourself, as the intention is pure and good.

Question 2: What is your body doing? Acknowledge how your body feels. If it is tight and stressed, try and shake it out a little. If you are able to leave the room for 30 seconds, or to go to the bathroom, this would be the perfect opportunity to have a private wiggle of your bottom, or wave of your arms. This releases the tension and the adrenaline that has built up, and helps to change your mood, because it is impossible to wiggle your bottom and still feel stressed. Lots of people do a power move, which is a punch with the fist in the air, or a more subtle clench of the fist, down by the side of the leg. Do whatever works for you, but a physical action will help change your emotions.

Question 3: What is your inner voice telling you? Talk to yourself like your best friend would talk to you. Tell yourself that you can do this, you are good at speaking, and you do know the answers. My favourite phrase when I'm nervous is, "You've got this!" And I talk to myself as if I am my own best friend.

This may sound like it's going to take a long time, but it really doesn't. You can literally do it in seconds. Practice as often as you can: focus, thoughts, and body. Picture your brain for focus, your lips for your inner voice/thoughts, and your arms for your body. Just changing one of these three things will help you, but changing all four will dramatically improve your emotions. You can go from scared to excited, in an instant—you just have to learn the technique. Throughout every part of the day, you are focused on something. Start to acknowledge this whenever you can. By practicing this, it will be much easier to tap into your focus, and then changing your focus will become easier and quicker.

To get a full page, full colour, print-ready copy of the strategies, visit www.themotivatedmummiesguidetoconfidence.com.

Practice What You Preach

Notes

Notes

Chapter 6

Food for Thought

Step 5: Be Healthy

"To eat is a necessity, but to eat intelligently is an art."
– François de La Rochefoucauld

I used to have a staple diet of cereal, pizza, and chocolate, so I know how it feels when someone says, "You need to eat carrot sticks instead of chocolate!" As if! We all know we need to eat fruit and vegetables, and limit our intake of junk, but it's not as easy as that. It would take more willpower than most of us have, to swap over just like that. When I went on the four-day seminar, Unleash the Power Within, in April 2017, I said to my new, amazing friend, Louise, "I love everything he said, but I'm not interested in the healthy eating and exercise side of it." I was happy with my unhealthy diet and couldn't see myself changing. Well, I'm sitting here writing this, with a bowl of freshly made kale crisps straight from the oven, and the healthiest smoothie you can imagine!

It took six months since the seminar to make the changes. I don't for one minute believe I changed my diet because Tony Robbins suggested it; I think I did it because I was ready. I was ready to be the best I can be, and we all know that doesn't include munching on greasy pizza every week, and family packs of chocolate! It doesn't matter how many people tell you that it's time to change, you will only do it when YOU are ready, and when your WHY is big enough.

Throughout my life, people had been suggesting that I eat healthier and exercise more, but being an average-sized woman, coming up to 40, I thought I was doing well enough. My chiropractor had given me some leaflets on certain vitamins and anti-inflammatory foods, which he said would help with my depression and anxiety, as well as my back pain; but I didn't take much notice. I bought the tablets and took them most days, but I didn't see any difference in my mental health, so I stopped. I guess I needed a slightly healthier diet alongside the tablets! One day, I decided I wasn't happy with my weight. It had crept up, and I didn't feel comfortable in any of my clothes. I definitely didn't like the spare tire that was hanging over my jeans when I sat down. I decided to ask a friend, who is a fitness instructor, how I could eat healthier. She gave me lots of great advice, but it was worlds away from where I was, and I just couldn't stick to it. Looking back now, I can see that I was addicted to sugar, which was why it was so hard to cut it out or dramatically reduce it.

When you're stuck in a rut, and feel down or depressed, there's no way on earth you are going to pick up a carrot stick and humus—it's just not going to happen. It doesn't matter if you know that's what you should be eating; the only thing you can manage to put in your mouth is quick and easy comfort food. Cereal was my food of choice when I was down—breakfast, lunch, and dinner, and sometimes an evening snack, if I was being good (instead of chocolate). I knew it wasn't a balanced diet, but it was good enough to keep me going, and the sugar content helped to cheer me up. For this reason, I am not going to tell you to go from your fast food to your celery stick overnight, but I will explain briefly why eating healthily helps with your mental health as well as your physical health and your confidence! You probably studied food health at school, but you may need a refresher. With all the fad diets around now, and the confusion of whether we should eat butter or margarine, or low fat or full fat, it's not surprising we are left in a spin!

Back to Basics

This part of the book is designed to remind you of how a balanced diet looks, and what your brain needs in order to perform well and keep you feeling mentally healthy. If you feel good, and you look good, your confidence soars. After reading this, you may like to take this further and find a health coach to work toward your goal quickly and productively, with a plan that speaks to you, and that would be amazing. Please ensure that your coach promotes a healthy, balanced diet, and not one that will just help you to lose weight. Most health coaches these days are all about mental wellbeing, and we are so lucky to live in a time when we have the internet at our fingertips to access such amazing information and great fitness coaches. Plus, with the added benefit of online courses, expert knowledge is often very accessible and affordable. There are a lot of eager coaches out there, ready to share their knowledge and help people live their best lives.
The information I am passing on has been found from numerous sites on the internet, and I consider it to be basic information and correct to the best of my knowledge, at the time of publication. Later on in this chapter, I will give suggestions on how to achieve this perfect balance of healthy eating by making small easy swaps, so don't get disheartened. Learn the knowledge, accept where you are, and then take some action.

> *"Healthy is not a size …*
> *It is a lifestyle."*
> *– Unknown*

Complex Carbohydrates

The body (and the brain) gets energy from a substance called glucose, which is found largely in carbohydrates. There are two forms of carbohydrates: simple and complex. Simple carbs are also referred to as sugars, and they can be found in their natural state in fruits and vegetables, and in their refined state in cakes, biscuits, jams, processed foods, and soft drinks. Simple carbs are metabolised and released into our blood quicker; hence the instant energy boost, which is the appeal for most people. Unfortunately, this energy expires as quickly as it comes, often leaving us feeling more tired and grumpy than before.

Complex carbs are turned into sugars and released into our blood in a slower, steadier, and more balanced way. This gives us a more stable energy, which lasts longer and won't negatively affect our blood sugar levels and moods. Complex carbs are also referred to as starch or starchy foods. They are present in their natural state in many foods, such as oats, brown rice, quinoa, potatoes, beans, and lentils, and in their refined state, mainly in processed foods. The best way to provide your body with a good quantity of complex carbs is to consume them in their most natural state. This way, they release energy slowly and help the brain to function in a stable way. For better concentration and mental performance, choose wholegrain foods (like wholemeal bread) instead of refined versions (like white bread).

Blood Sugar Levels

Blood sugar fluctuations can be an important factor in anxiety and mood swings. In short, when we eat a sugar (simple carbohydrate), our blood sugar quickly goes up, and our body then produces insulin, which drops our blood sugar quickly back down again, creating a *crash* or *slump* in blood sugar. This, in turn, can make our energy *crash* or *slump*. This crash can make us feel fatigued and lightheaded, and can affect our concentration, and produce other symptoms, such as panic. This can very quickly trigger our fight or flight response. The symptoms intensify, and the anxiety cycle is started. All this is very subtle; you are not going to eat a Mars bar and then, 20 minutes later, run around in a blind panic! The effects of food on our systems are not usually obvious, although in some cases, it is easier to see than in others. A way you can combat the effects of this rollercoaster of blood sugar levels is to eat fewer simple carbs (sugars, white grains, processed starches), and eat more complex carbohydrates (whole grains) and protein (meats, fish, eggs, etc.). It is advised that you get half your daily energy needs from carbohydrates. Simple carbs/refined sugars should make up just 11% of your daily diet; however, research shows that the average adult man has a daily intake of refined sugars of 13.6%, and the average child's is 16%! I wonder if these statistics have any connection to the shocking rise of children with anxiety these days.

The important things to remember for a good blood sugar balance is:

- Eat a protein with your carbohydrate.
- Aim for 40–50% of your calorie intake to be from carbs.
- Reduce the amount of simple carbs you eat.
- Choose unrefined carbs whenever you can.
- Do not cut them out of your diet completely; they are important.

> *"A healthy outside starts from the inside."*
> – Robert Urich

Protein

Protein provides us with the raw materials that make up all of our body tissues. Our organs, muscles, nails, hair, hormones, and blood cells are all made from protein (along with other more technical bits); and protein is made up of amino acids. The brain and its long spidery neurons are essentially made of fat, but they communicate with each other via proteins. The hormones and enzymes that cause chemical changes and control all body processes are also made of protein. Key neurotransmitters are made from amino acids (obtained from protein), so protein is very important for our diet.

Almost all complete proteins come from animal sources. This means that they contain all of the essential amino acids and many of the nonessential ones too. Most plant sources are incomplete; therefore, anyone following a vegetarian or vegan diet needs to ensure that they are careful to combine food sources so that they get all the amino acids each day. Serious physical and mental health issues can arise from a lack of essential amino acids in the body. To ensure that you are getting enough protein in your diet to maintain physical and mental health, make sure you include a portion of protein in every meal. Add extras, such as eggs, tuna, chicken, or cheese to a salad (with healthy fats from avocado, eggs, and olive oil to ensure that the fat-soluble vitamins can be absorbed). Combine lentils or beans with rice to get the full complement of essential amino acids, and don't consider fruit salad to be a meal!

Neurotransmitters are a chemical substance, which is released at the end of a nerve fibre. The nerve fibres connect via this substance, which allows communication from one nerve to another, or to a muscle fibre or some other structure.

Neurotransmitters in the brain, which regulate our moods, are made from amino acids. Some of these amino acids come from what we eat and drink. For example, the neurotransmitter, serotonin, which helps us feel content and is important for sleep, is made from the amino acid, tryptophan, found in milk, oats, and other foods. This is probably why many mothers used to give their child a glass of warm milk before bed. These neurotransmitters are involved in mood, sleep, nervous system function, anxiety, sexual function, immune function, alertness, motivation, concentration, memory, learning, appetite, blood pressure, and more. Additionally, research has linked major depression with altered levels of the amino acid's glutamic acid and aspartic acid, as well as other amino acids such as serine and glycine. If your body is lacking in these amino acids, then you will not be able to make adequate amounts of these important neurotransmitters, and your mental health will suffer. This also hugely affects your confidence and self-esteem.

"The food you eat really can affect your mood. For a good night's sleep, choose food and drink rich in tryptophan, such as a milky drink before bed."

Vitamins and Minerals

Vitamins and minerals are important for the functioning of your whole body. The brain uses vitamins and minerals to help perform vital tasks. A vitamin or mineral shortage can affect your mood, as well as other brain functions. Vitamins such as folate and B12 support the healthy function of the nervous system. A deficiency in either of these vitamins can cause a wide range of problems, including:

- memory problems
- fatigue
- muscle weakness
- pins and needles
- psychological problems
- mouth ulcers

If you are suffering from low mood or depression, which is out of character, it could be worth asking your doctor to check your vitamin D levels, as I have known many women who have needed a vitamin D injection to boost their supplies, and this has worked wonders.

Good Fats

The *dry weight* of the brain is about 60% fats, and a fifth of this fat is made from the essential fatty acids, omega-3 and omega-6. Essential fatty acids cannot be made by the body, so they have to come from the diet, unlike nonessential amino acids, which can be made by the body. You must have all amino acids so your body can build the wide variety of proteins it needs to repair, maintain, and aid growth of the cells. Most of us eat much more omega-6 (found in poultry, eggs, avocado, and nuts) than omega-3 (found in oily fish; seeds, especially flax seeds; and nuts, especially walnuts), but we do need both.

Your brain is made of 60% good fats!

However, trans fats, also known as hydrogenated fats, are particularly bad for the brain, because they stop essential fatty acids from doing their work effectively. They are found in many ready-made foods, like cakes and biscuits. Check labels for hydrogenated fat or oil, and avoid these foods where possible.

"The brain represents only 2% of an adult's weight, but it uses 20% of the energy produced by the body."

Food and Drink to Boost Your Brain

There are some foods that seem to be particularly good for our brains, when eaten as part of a balanced diet.

- Extra virgin olive oil: This is a healthy source of fat in the diet, and it can help reduce cholesterol levels and blood pressure. Some studies have linked olive oil with a lower risk of ischaemic stroke, cognitive impairment, and Alzheimer's disease.
- Oily fish (salmon, herring, mackerel): This is an excellent source of omega 3, which your brain needs to stay healthy.
- Berries and other deep-coloured fruits and vegetables (strawberries, blueberries, blackberries, spinach, beetroot, beans): These foods are high in antioxidants, which help guard against disease by protecting cells in the body and brain from damage.
- Foods containing good fats: Foods containing polyunsaturated fatty acids (nuts, seeds, fish, leafy green vegetables) and monounsaturated fatty acids (extra virgin olive oil, avocados, nuts) may reduce your risk of both depression and dementia.

Food for Thought

- Dark chocolate: (yay!) It contains high levels of antioxidants, although it is also high in sugar and fat. One small piece of dark chocolate per day is enough to get the antioxidant benefit.
- Green tea: This is another rich source of antioxidants.

As well as *what* you eat, *when* you eat is also important. Eating regular meals will help you to maintain steady energy levels. In particular, you should also try to eat breakfast, as this will help your concentration and mental performance throughout the day.

Dark chocolate has high levels of antioxidants. Swap milk chocolate for dark chocolate, and you will be healthier; plus, it's not as sweet, so it's easier to put down.

Healthy swaps and tips:

- Swap to water as often as you can. This will not only save you lots of money, but it is great for your skin, helping you to look younger, as well as flooding your body with the hydration it needs.
- Cut down on bread, wheat, and gluten. You can swap to gluten-free, or find alternatives to sandwiches.
- Buy products with no added sugar/salt, as often as you can. A lot of our favourite brands are offering this now.
- Look at shop-owned brands and value foods; these often have less calories than the top brands, and they are cheaper.
- Try baking your own crisps and chips. You might be surprised at how tasty they are!
- Add one healthy food a week to your menu. If you stick with it, your tastes buds will grow to tolerate and even enjoy the taste. I did this with green tea, and now I hardly ever have English Breakfast tea bags.
- Make a gradual swap from cows' milk to an alternative. You can start by pouring half-and-half on your cereals.

- Eat as much non-processed food as possible (i.e. Use tinned tomatoes and spices instead of tinned Bolognese sauces.). Our bodies can absorb and use non-processed food much easier. This alone can help you lose excess weight.
- Reduce portion sizes.
- Eat little and often, so you don't get hungry and make poor decisions.
- If you or your children do not like the texture of healthy food, blitz it up into a smoothie.
- Drink lots of fluids, preferably water; it makes you feel fuller, and sometimes you are not hungry, just thirsty.
- Try making homemade biscuits and cakes, and swap butter for coconut oil. There are plenty of recipes on the internet to try.
- Swap breakfast cereals for porridge or protein such as eggs or a healthy smoothie.
- Reduce any added sugar in food or in drinks, a little at a time, and one day, you will wonder how you ever had sugar in your tea to start with.
- Try cacao powder to get your chocolate fix; it's full of magnesium, fibre, protein, iron, and potassium, plus it is 100% organic, and great in a smoothie or mixed with natural yogurt.
- Try hot water and a squeeze of lemon every morning. Having an alkaline body has been proven to reduce the chances of getting cancer, and it also promotes healthy digestion and weight loss.

"By cleansing your body on a regular basis, and eliminating as many toxins as possible from your environment, your body can begin to heal itself, prevent disease, and become stronger and more resilient than you ever dreamed possible!"
– Dr. Edward Group III

There are many detox plans out on the market, and as I personally will not promote them, I do see the benefits of detoxing your body. We all have little bugs in our bellies, and without getting technical, these bugs crave sugary *bad* food, so even if we are trying to be good, our body is craving it, and that is hard to ignore! You can do a simple (but not easy) detox very cheaply with water and lemons. Drink warm boiled water with half a lemon squeezed into it, 3 times a day, and plenty of water in between. You can add apple cider vinegar for extra effects. Stop all caffeine and sugary foods for 4 days while you do this, and if you survive (the first day is the hardest, as your body screams for what it knows), then you will be free of the nasty little craving bugs, and the rest of your healthy eating plan will be so much easier.

Exercising with Kids

Many of you are very busy, and the thought of adding in an exercise routine is more than you can bear—just one more task on your to-do list! If you do not have spare time at the moment, or you just do not want to use your spare time to exercise, that's fine; I'm going to offer you some suggestions for how you can incorporate it into your family life. This way, you are still getting healthier and exercising, and you are being a great role model for your children, without compromising anything else. It is really important that you show your children the value of a healthy lifestyle, and lead them down a path that will really benefit them throughout their life. As we have spoken of before, we tend to follow what we have seen, and we copy many family traditions and behaviours.

But as times have changed, we have changed with them, so even if we did have a very active and healthy upbringing, we may not be doing that for our children, purely because we have so much more to fit in these days. Don't let this be an excuse though. There is always time to prioritise your health, and there is always time to spend with your children if you really want to. I know that might sound a bit harsh, especially if you are reading this and you are a single mum with a full time job. As busy as you are, you can still prioritise your children and your health at some point throughout the day. Children do not need constant attention, but they do need quality time. Even a mum working all the hours God sends can still give their child 100% of their attention at some point during the week. I talk about priorities and time management in my transformation group, so if you are struggling to find the time to live your life the way you want to live it, then look up The Motivated Mummies transformation group, and allow me to help you find that special time to spend with your family, before it's too late.

When my two children were 3 years old and 6 months old, their dad moved out, and I was left to raise them alone and keep a roof over our heads. I worked bloody hard to pay for the mortgage by myself, and to have everything else we needed. I was emotionally and physically shattered most of the time, but one of the benefits of being a single mum was that I had no one walking in at the end of the day, moaning about how messy the house was. I answered to myself only. This was a huge plus to me. I did, of course, keep the house clean, but it was not my first priority. I was a qualified nursery nurse, and I knew the importance of play with children, so I made sure I prioritised some quality time with them. Looking back now, I could have done better, but at the time, with the knowledge I had, it was the best I could do. One of the reasons I have set up The Motivated Mummies transformation group is so that other mums don't have wasted time, and look back with regret. I now know that I have the ability to help mums create a great work life balance, so they never have to look back in regret, or with guilt that they didn't do their best.

"In my career, there are many things I've won and many things I've achieved, but for me, my greatest achievement is my children and my family. It's about being a good father, a good husband, and just being connected to family as much as possible."
– David Beckham

ACTION

Let's look at some of the ways that you can exercise whilst spending quality time with your children too:

- Pillow fighting
- Jumping on the trampoline
- Playing chase
- Jogging around the local park
- Walking together
- Skipping with a rope
- Playing football, rounders, rugby
- Tag tickle
- Hunt the thimble on a timer
- *Keepy up* with a ball or balloon
- Water fight
- Swimming
- Tree climbing
- Digging at the beach
- Family yoga in the garden
- Gardening
- Riding bikes
- Jogging while children ride their bikes

These are just a few suggestions, and I am sure you can think of more. Anything that gets you breathing heavily, your heart pumping harder, and a bit of a sweat on, is exercise. Imagine if you incorporated this into your life three times a week. Your children would get more quality time with you, you would all be fitter, and you would be a happier, tighter family through the bonding activities. These games do not have to be long. They can be if you have time and energy, but if not, just start with ten minutes. My biggest advice, if you are doing this with young children, is to please tell them what is happening. If it will be ten minutes, then tell them it's ten minutes; otherwise, from their point of view, Mum comes to play, they have a great time, and then

Mum leaves when they want to continue the fun. Pre warn them so you do not get grief afterwards. I like to set a timer: "Come on kids, I have 10 minutes while the potatoes are cooking, so let's set the timer and play chase in the garden for 10 minutes." This way, they know why you are playing then (and not later when you are working), you have time, they know how long to expect you to play, they know it will end, and after that, you'll be busy again. They may still crave your attention afterwards, but if you make this a habit, they will learn that there are times when Mum plays, and times when she needs to be left alone. How often do you say to your child, "I need you to be quiet now while I'm on the phone for 10 minutes," or, "I need to work now, so please don't interrupt me?" Opposed to how many times you say, "Hey, let's play for 10 minutes." I know what I hear said most.

> *"We don't stop playing because we grow old;*
> *we grow old because we stop playing."*
> *– George Bernard Shaw*

By playing and doing physical activities with your children, you are giving them the quality time they need and deserve, and you are wearing them out too! I always say to mums of young children, who work from home, to take their child out first. Let them have fresh air and exercise, and THEN come home and ask them to play quietly while you work—never the other way around. In the morning, they have all this energy from a good night's sleep, and they have missed you. They are too young and too egocentric (only think of themselves) to understand, "Let Mummy just work, and then I'll take you out." Rearrange your working day so you get your exercise first with your child. This is also a great way to boost yourself for the day; you will be much more energised after a physical workout, and you will be more productive.

> *"Those who think they have no time for exercise will*
> *sooner or later have to find time for illness."*
> *– Edward Stanley*

Inspirational Ladies

As mums, we have one thing in common: We all have children—and generally, that is where the comparison ends. Each one of you reading this will have a completely different life to the next. You have your own circumstances and your own routines. I have been lucky enough to find several mums who have been happy to share their stories with you, in hopes of inspiring you to take action, if you haven't already, and find an exercise or healthy eating plan that suits you and your family. Each one of these ladies is unique. Some have young children, and some have older children; some ladies have time, and some others have found time. These ladies all have different lives, with all different situations, and some have had serious problems that they've overcome. I haven't just chosen mums with one child, who are ladies of leisure; oh no, one lady has 6 children, and we have a single mum. Some have health problems, and some have been in very dark places. Others have unique and interesting hobbies that keep them fit—we have a wide selection. I am so grateful to each and every one of them, and so glad that they have seen an increase in their confidence by taking action and improving their own health in some way or another. Hopefully, you will read their stories and be able to relate to at least one of them, allowing them to lift you up and realise that anything is possible….

Exhausted, fed up, bored, unhappy, overweight, worthless, and no doubt depressed—that's how I felt after being at home with the kids for twelve years! Who even was I anymore??! I'm sure this sounds familiar to many women.

 I just didn't feel like the confident, happy, funny, slim person I once was. I knew things had to change, but I wasn't sure how! All I knew was that I needed to get a job, lose weight, and find myself. But I hadn't been in the workplace for over twelve years, and I hated the idea of going to a gym!

One day, as I was scrolling through Groupon, I saw something that caught my eye—Bellydance Bootcamp!! It was just staring at me, for only £8! I loved dancing!! I remembered how, many years ago, I was on holiday in Turkey, and a belly dancer chose me to stay on the dance floor with her and move how she was moving (which I could do very easily as I was only twenty something, flexible, and a size 8!). I was blown away by the dance style, but back then, it never even occurred to me that you could learn it!!! However, I knew I couldn't move like that anymore, but I wanted to force myself to get out and do something for me!

I was brave enough to purchase this £8 deal, but was I brave enough to go on my own?? I only ever went to things with a friend.

Well, the day came, and I stood at the door, telling myself that if I saw lots of young, slim women, I would just turn around and leave! But to my surprise, it was women of all shapes and sizes, young and old. I had an amazing time! I was buzzing after the class. I decided straight away that I would join classes and do something for myself that I enjoyed.

I quickly made friends and started noticing how happy I was, and I was looking forward to classes every week. I also joined a local Zumba class. I was feeling a bit braver. I also joined Tropic skincare, through a friend, and began a real journey in building my self-confidence again. I was getting fitter (maybe not slimmer), and I was feeling more myself again. I loved that I was moving my body, and I always felt great after a class. With belly dancing, I was learning more and more about it, with different styles and moves. Classes were never focused on age or body size; it was all about how you embraced the way your body moved. I was even doing stage performances with my classmates, which really gave me a boost. I'd done it before in my youth, and I wanted to feel the buzz and excitement again! I'll never forget that surge of adrenaline, and the self-esteem boost I got after the first performance.

Then, one day, I just sat back and thought for a moment: I was happy! I wasn't thinking about my problems, marriage, or even my weight. I was never going to be a size 8 again, and I honestly didn't want to be. I was comfortable being the size 14 that I was. Don't get me wrong; it would be nice to lose a bit more around the waistline, but it wasn't bothering me the way it did before. I was getting compliments about how I looked, and people wanted to know how I was always so happy! I was inspiring ladies around me to do things that made them happy! That gave me the biggest confidence boost!

Fast forward four years to present day, and that bored, unhappy, worthless, overweight person is a distant memory. Don't get me wrong; I still have days where I feel flat, unmotivated, and not very confident. But I also know that I don't want to be that other person ever again!! Dancing gave me back my feel-good factor, and I never want to lose it! I never lost any major weight, and that's okay; I guess none of us are entirely satisfied in that department anyway. But I strive to be as healthy as I can (unless I see cake). I'm way more confident than I ever was in my life! I've gone from a beginner to an advanced level, in four years. I've performed well over 10 times now with my dance groups. I've yet to do my first solo performance, which I know I will do soon. I do 3–4 hours of belly dance classes a week, and Zumba and yoga too!

I never want to stop dancing! I'd like to teach belly dancing one day. I'm not sure if I'll ever get there, but I'm going to have fun trying. And to think it all started with an £8 Groupon deal!

Nayan Mistry
Santa Maria Bellydance Academy

I signed up to the UWCB Boxing event for a few reasons: I like to challenge myself with new things; it raises money for cancer research, which like most people these days, cancer has taken too many loved ones from me; and I wanted to get fit.

I was so nervous on the first training day, to the point that my anxiety nearly made me turn and run back out the door. Thankfully, I didn't turn and run away.

The coaches were amazing: Sally and Colin, husband and wife, who run Lions gym, in Watford. They were so encouraging, in every way possible, and they cared as much about your mental health as your physical health. Sally, Colin, and their whole team of coaching staff became like family. I looked forward to every training session, even on the days when I may have felt nervous about what we were doing—like when you first get in the ring and start sparring with someone else.

It did take up a lot of my time, as any spare time I had, I wanted to train so that I was fit for fight night. The children didn't mind, as they knew how important it was to me, and I explained that it was only 3 months of intense training. My son would sometimes come and join me, punching the punch bags a few times, until he was bored, and then he would go back to his Xbox. His teacher come up to me after school and told me that he had been telling her all about my boxing and running that I do, and that I'm really strong, which put a massive smile on my face. My fight was put up on YouTube, and I was pleasantly surprised when my daughter wanted to show her friend my fight. My daughter does not normally show much interest in what I do (exercise wise).

UWCB boxing was by far one of the best things I have ever done, and I would highly recommend it to anyone!! It's not what you think; everyone I met was so kind and caring, even the big, heavyweight men. It was an amazing, life changing experience.

I was the strongest and fittest I've ever been, and I felt very confident in myself, and happy. I had a newfound family at the boxing gym, and I made some fantastic friendships along the way.

My children were proud of me and what I achieved. We raised a great amount of money for cancer research as well.

I would do it again!

On to my next challenge: Prudential London bike ride, 100 miles.

Lisa Huse

After giving birth to my first child in 2010, I didn't feel like myself anymore. My body had changed so drastically, and I seemed to be putting on more weight, no matter how much I exercised. I couldn't fit back into my pre-pregnancy jeans, and I had to go shopping for bigger pant sizes. This caused a major decline in my confidence and my feelings of self-worth. I struggled to find motivation to go out into public, even to do something as simple as grocery shopping. Honestly, I felt hopeless, and I had lost a lot of my joy and zest for life.

In 2012, I was diagnosed with Hashimoto's Hypothyroidism, an autoimmune disease in which your immune system attacks your thyroid. Some of my symptoms included (but were not limited to) the following: weight gain, extreme tiredness, fatigue, depression, achy joints, slow heart rate, brain fog, and mental and emotional stress. Most days, my train of irrational thoughts led me to bawling my eyes out on the floor. Even though doctors put me on medication, it wasn't making me feel any better.

After several years of feeling sick and sorry for myself, a light bulb turned on in my brain. When I finally decided that I was going to take my health into my own hands, everything changed. I understood that in order to change my current state of health, I had to take massive action and stop waiting around for a miracle pill. Slowly but surely, through changing my nutrition, I started to take my life back! Through removing certain foods from my diet, and adding nutrient-rich foods,

I have gained so much mental clarity, which has allowed me to look at myself in a whole new light.

Fast forward to today (2019)…I am back down to the size I was in high school, which I never thought was possible. By learning new healthy habits, not only have I lost physical weight, but I've also lost a lot of mental weight. I've minimized a lot of my symptoms, feel more energy, and have my spark back! I can't even truly explain what this has done for my confidence. All I know is that today I am paying it forward by helping other mamas gain their health and their life back. Every woman deserves to feel confident in her own body, and have the enthusiasm to pursue her own dreams.

No matter what you are going through, there is hope and there is a solution. Solutions often take time and perseverance. I have hit many stumbling blocks on my road to health, and my journey is still far from over. However, no matter how many times I fail, I keep getting back up and keep trying. Experiencing failure, learning from those failures, and moving forward with a new strategy is the only way success eventually occurs. My husband always says that "your problems are not unique." You are unique as a person, but your problems are not. Someone, somewhere in the world, has gone through the same and/or similar situation as you are going through right now. You don't have to suffer alone. We are stronger and better together. Ultimately, if you find a way to make your health a priority, you will find yourself motivated and thriving in all other areas of your life.

Bridget Du Haime (Health & Life Coach)
www.DHResultsCoaching.com

Giving Fags the Axe

I started smoking as an older teenager, for all the wrong reasons, and didn't really enjoy smoking. When my daughter was a young toddler, I was smoking a pack a day. I rationalized that it helped me relax from my stressful life. I was a single mom, worked two jobs, was very physically active, and was trying to raise my daughter to be a strong little girl. I also told myself that it helped me socialize with other people. I had it so, so wrong. I had a scare with asthma that sent me to the hospital when she was 3, and I was there for three days. All the while, my family—bless them—cared for my daughter around the clock. In those three days, I had nothing but time to think about what I was doing with my life, and how unhappy I was. Smoking was at the top of the list of harmful things, both for my health and the time it was taking me away from my daughter. I wouldn't smoke around her; I'd take the long way to day care to pick her up so I could have one more. I'd leave her in the living room watching TV, to step out onto the porch. Then, there I was, hospitalized on oxygen and round the clock breathing treatments. For three whole days, I only got to see her for the few little bits of time my family could bring her during visiting hours.

I quit cold turkey!

I made the decision, and just quit. It was rough at first, but as each day passed, it was easier and easier. I also discovered a newfound confidence in myself that I was able to give it up like that. If I could do this, what else could I do? I was more present and focused with my daughter; I was more patient, attentive, and relaxed. It only made life better. My daughter is a grown woman now, and full of independence and excitement for all life has to offer. I haven't had a single fag since then (going on 17 years now), and I attribute quitting smoking to the confidence boost it gave me to try other things in my life. My change gave her a mother who was a great role model, and a relationship with me that she could trust to take leaps of faith herself, knowing I was going to be around to catch her. When there's something I want to accomplish, but it feels insurmountable, I remember when I quit smoking, as evidence that I CAN do this despite the obstacles.

Heather Humphries

My name is Samantha Francis, and I am a coach/mentor, therapist, and best-selling author. More importantly, I am a mum of two girls, aged 11 and 7. My relationship with my body and exercise has often been an arduous one since my teens, but it has been a journey where I have learned to develop confidence over the years, not only in my body but in myself too. My journey into health and exercise started after the birth of my eldest. I was physically in pain due to birth trauma, and was not able to use my body properly without a struggle. I was also severely depressed. I was a size 14 and miserable. I decided to change my life by starting to exercise, as I knew the benefits for not just my body but my mind too. I fit it in and made it an important part of my day, just like brushing my teeth or eating. I started off exercising quite heavily for about an hour a day in my living room, using workout programmes and free workouts on YouTube, etc., and the weight soon fell off, and my confidence started to grow.

It was easier to start loving what I was seeing on the outside, before I could love me for me, on the inside. Yet that still wasn't enough for me. I still felt empty, so I continued my regime, upping it to sometimes two hours a day, and hardly eating in order to lose more, which I did, but I soon realised that I was using it as a way of control, as I felt everything else in my life was out of control. Luckily, I caught myself early. Instead, I decided that it was more important for my children and me to see me attain the confidence and self-worth that I needed more so than a thin body. I never wanted my children to think that food/exercise was a punishment, or that using it as a way of keeping control was okay.

I resumed working out on a daily basis, for 20–30 minutes, over the years, and showed my girls how important it was to fit it in and make it important. They often joined me and still do! My relationship with exercise increased my positivity and happiness in myself. I felt accomplished after every workout, and that was the buzz and incentive to push me forward. I, of course, sorted the other areas of my life out too, but my mood significantly lifted, and I found my body changing into a stronger version of what it was before. I went from punishing my body to actually loving it and being proud of what it has gone through and how far it has come!

Samantha Francis
https://www.facebook.com/Soulholisticshealing/

In May 2016, I walked into a weight watchers' group. I'd been there many times before, but I knew this time would be the hardest, and as I weighed in at 30st4lb, I was devastated. So many emotions went through me, mostly shame and embarrassment, as I finally saw what I had been denying to myself for a long time. Unfortunately, in the few months following joining WW, my family and I faced homelessness, as our landlord was selling the house we lived in and, as we were unable to find another landlord who would rent to a family with 5 children, we were forced by our local council to wait for the bailiffs to evict us before we would be housed.

Unsure of when this might be, I ignored some worrying symptoms that I had been having. After a month of drinking up to 30 pints of water a day, my husband came home from work one day, and my eyes couldn't focus on him properly. As I suspected, I was quickly diagnosed with type 2 diabetes, but the doctors struggled to get my blood sugar levels under control, and I had to stay overnight in hospital and was injecting myself several times daily with insulin. A week after being in hospital, my family was finally evicted at the end of August and placed in temporary accommodation, 25 miles from our hometown. I had to commute my children to school every day, leaving at 6am to ensure they were on time, and not returning until 7pm every day. This wasn't a great time to be eating healthily, but I tried my best until we were housed permanently in October. This whole period left me feeling very down and out of control. It's hard to motivate yourself when you're feeling like this, but I just kept doing the little things that I could.

Finally, in January 2017, I weighed in after Christmas, expecting to have gained, but I hadn't. Around that time, I had a routine diabetes eye examination, during which I was told that I have a coiled blood vessel in one of my eyes, and that if my blood pressure or blood sugar levels weren't well controlled, it could burst and I would go blind! This really shook me into reality, and I knew then that I had to take back the control. I stopped feeling sorry for myself and started to move more. Until then, the only exercise I did was walking from my car to the kids' school and back again, twice a day. There was a hill I would drive on every day, and one day I parked at the bottom, put a song on my iPod, and walked up the hill as far as I could for one song. It was so hard! But I did it again the next day, and the day after that! I kept walking all through January and February.

In March, I signed up for Race for Life, which would be in May. I decided I would try and run it, so I started the Couch to 5k programme. That was really tough, more emotionally than anything else, at first. I would only run at 5:30 in the morning so that it would still be dark outside, and I was less likely to be seen! My confidence slowly grew, and thanks to the mornings getting lighter, I had to start running in the daylight!! At the end of April, I joined a Back to Netball group. That was really hard, as I was clearly the most overweight person there, not to mention the most unfit. I had seen the poster for it back in January but didn't have the courage to join then, but it was the best decision I ever made! I made so many friends through the group that I joined another group that ran in summer when the first one wasn't on. I now go to 3 different sessions a week and have such a great time.

I also joined an online women's only fitness group called Callender Girls, which focuses on helping women to increase their fitness and be the best that they can be. Through that programme, my confidence has increased immeasurably. It's been almost three years since I first decided to lose weight. My doctor no longer considers me diabetic, as my blood sugar levels are consistently normal without medication. Along the way, I've had to be selfish at times and do what I felt was best for me, but finding a fun fitness activity like Netball was key to helping me be successful. I've lost about 14 stone so far, and my journey hasn't finished yet.

Louvaine Hunt

Losing weight massively improved my confidence and wellbeing!

Up until pregnancy, I'd always been quite slim and was fairly into my fitness. I put a lot of weight on over the 9 months. I'd gone from 9 to 12 stones on the scales very quickly! It had a huge effect on my confidence, happiness, and well-being. I felt drained most of the time, I didn't feel confident in the way I looked, my inner dialogue was very negative, and I felt like I would never get my old body back.

I found it quite hard to stay focused to lose it again. I would yo-yo diet and go up and down on the scales. I found myself in a negative cycle of restriction, craving foods I wasn't supposed to have, and negative self-talk. I would get so far, fail, beat myself up, *give up*, and pile it all back on again! I ended up suffering from depression, and my marriage broke down.

I worked for 5 years on my own personal development and decided to change my whole way of thinking toward food and dieting, and most importantly, toward myself.

I wanted to concentrate on taking easy, baby steps, which felt good to me. The compound effect started to work, and I finally started to stop beating myself up, and became a lot kinder to myself.

I concentrated on various different mindset techniques and used these tools consistently until I reached my target weight. It was surprisingly easy, and fun, once I managed to make the shift in my mind, and view things in a different way.

When the weight finally came off again, I felt far more confident in myself, I had so much more energy, I felt so light, and I started to feel like myself again. I found that I was less hungry, and I didn't stress over food anymore, and cravings also stopped. Because of this, I felt happier, and the knock-on effect was that I became more successful in other areas of my life too.

I decided to help other people and teach them how to do the same, as I knew there must be a lot of other people going through the same thing. I became a life coach and set up a 6-week online Mindset for Weight Loss coaching course. I'm so happy now to be able to share with other people the tools and techniques to turn their lives around and finally get to their target weight and keep it off. There are a lot of fantastic weight loss products and exercise plans out there; however, I found that most of them seemed to lack training the mind first, and that's ultimately where it starts. I believe you can change anything when you change your thinking!

Mairi Holden
www.pinkjazz.co.uk

How confidence grows when you make a change in your eating patterns and/or your exercise

After giving birth to my son, in August 2017, my confidence was at the lowest point in my life. Being pregnant was no longer an excuse for looking *chubby* or overweight. I became obsessed with how others viewed me. When I looked in the mirror, I did not recognise the person looking back at me. I saw an out-of-shape person forced into size 10 clothes that no longer fit her—an unhappy, tired person with no self-love. That person was me.

After a few weeks of self-pity—at which point I had mostly recovered from my C-section—I decided it was time to take action and make positive changes. This was a huge turning point in my life, and one that I am very grateful for. Growing up, I was always referred to as *skinny* or *underweight*, labels which then were somehow normalised into a compliment, which is what I saw them as. Was I healthy? Absolutely not. I lacked basic nutrients such as vitamin C and iron. I was addicted to sugar; in fact, most of my calories came from simple carbohydrates and sugar. At the time, I viewed cereal as healthy, and I had no idea how much sugar was actually in fruit juice. No one knew of my sugar addiction because, truth be told, we all had an unhealthy relationship with added sugar—we just didn't know it.

My post-partum weight-loss journey started off by simply tracking my calories; calories in vs calories out—simple. That, and returning to the gym three times a week. It was going well—it worked. However, after 3 weeks I could no longer put up with the constant tiredness and hunger. My willpower was deteriorating, and I knew something needed to change. To lose weight, you need to eat in a calorie deficit, but not all calories are the same. I soon realised that chocolates and crisps were not providing me with the nutrients I needed—they were high in calories and did not fill me up. It was at this point, after endless amounts of research into different diets, such as juicing and keto, that a high protein, no added sugar lifestyle was the perfect choice for me. My body needed high amounts of protein to aid muscle recovery, as I had started powerlifting. Protein is also low in calories and keeps you feeling full for longer, which made it the perfect food to aid my weight loss and healthy eating.

Cutting out sugar was a slow and tough process, but it was by far the best decision I had ever made. I now have more energy and can eat food that is beneficial to my body, such as vegetables and complex carbohydrates. I no longer have sugar cravings or allow my desire for sugar to dictate irrational choices that I used to make on impulse, such as binge eating on desserts. I was hungry, but instead of eating a home cooked, healthy meal, I would choose to consume a dessert, leaving me fatigued, hungry, and craving more sugar. Breaking from this vicious cycle of bad choices, and making new, healthier choices gave me the confidence I did not know was possible to attain.

My healthy eating lifestyle, combined with my new interests in powerlifting and boxing, gave me a sense of direction of where life was heading, and it gave me strength and purpose. The feeling of deadlifting 90kg for repetitions is truly indescribable. I felt in control and powerful. But more importantly, I felt happy—happy with the journey I had embarked on thus far, and happy with the obstacles I had overcome, and happy with the progress I had made. I write this now as a personal trainer and boxing instructor, nineteen months after giving birth to my beautiful son, and I am overjoyed that I can turn my passion of health and fitness into helping others make physical and mental changes. Making these healthier lifestyle choices made me who I am today, and I hope others gain confidence when making changes to their own eating habits and exercise regimes.

Maryam Akram
www.lifteverest.com

The pains started in my 4th pregnancy. I struggled to sit on the floor, which was something I did without thinking before. I put it down to pregnancy and didn't think anything of it. Fast forward to my 5th pregnancy, and I was in agony. I struggled with daily tasks. Literally, everything I did caused me pain—from walking to standing, to getting in and out of the car. Even turning over in bed was painful. I couldn't lift anything heavy; even pushing a supermarket trolley was impossible. Some days were a struggle to get through, and my quality of life had been affected. I was affected both mentally and physically. I went to see the doctor so many times. I told the doctor that something was wrong, and that I felt like the baby was just going to fall out. She took no notice and said it was normal, as I had lots of children!

So, along comes pregnancy number 6. I was in agony (remember, I hadn't been diagnosed yet). I went to see the doctor again and again.

In the end, I told her that I have SPD—Symphysis Pubis Dysfunction (that was what it was called back in those days). I did lots of research to come to this conclusion myself, and contacted support groups online for advice. I had hydrotherapy sessions whilst pregnant. I could barely move. After giving birth, I had physiotherapy sessions. I went to the chiropractor for 2 and a half years. My pelvis kept on moving out of place. Pelvic girdle pain is real! If I lost my footing, I would be in agony for days; my pubic bones would hurt. Being in constant pain was exhausting. It wasn't something that others could see physically, so others often didn't understand what I was going through.

I decided that I had to help myself. I started walking, and I would be in agony and would often cry. But I kept on moving. I registered for the Race for Life, and I was scared that I wouldn't be able to take part. I increased my walking and kept on moving. I would have setbacks (the hot water bottle and ice pack were my best friends!), but I completed the Race for Life with my children, and I cried with joy. I power walked and couldn't believe that I had done it. I was so proud of myself.

One afternoon, I had gone for a walk with one of my children, and I nearly fainted. I had to sit down in the street, and that's when the penny dropped for me. I knew I had to really look after myself. Being a mum, we often don't look after ourselves, but I knew that if I didn't look after myself, who would look after my children? After a blood test, I was told that I had prediabetes. So, I went on a juice fast for 30 days (I know some people don't like juice fasts, but I had to take drastic action.). I was tested again and no longer had prediabetes.

I joined a Pilates class with a trained physiotherapist to strengthen my core. When I would come home, I would put ice on my back, as I knew I would be in pain after the class. I kept on going to the class for 1 and a half years, and I kept on walking. I wore my shoes out!

I started doing fitness blender classes at home, and I bought a few of their programmes. I stuck to the low impact workouts. I decided to do a few more juice fasts, as I wanted to lose weight and become stronger before my 40th birthday. I was on a high! I was taking care of myself because I had to. My children and husband always supported me and encouraged me to keep on going. They all helped when I was struggling with pain or if I had setbacks.

It took me 10 years to feel ready to go to the gym. I was scared; I didn't want to hurt myself using the equipment. I went to an induction class, and the personal trainer told me to do the exercises that I enjoy; otherwise, I would stop going. That was the best advice I was given, and that's exactly what I did. I built up my confidence and physical fitness on the gym floor before having the confidence to attend classes. The classes were fun. I went to circuits, abs, fat-burn, Pilates, and even Zumba, amongst others. In one of the circuit classes, I thought I was Rocky, and started skipping and skipping… My pelvic girdle pain came back, and it triggered memories for me. I didn't want to go backward; I had worked hard to move forward. I then went to see another chiropractor, and she confirmed that my pelvis had indeed moved. I've had 6 sessions with her and feel much better now.

I knew I had to calm down, as I did actually become a gym addict, and when I started, I would jump on the scale every month and analyse my fat percentage. I would wonder why it had gone up or down. Now, going to the gym isn't about weight at all. It is about being healthy and strong. I never go on the scale, as I actually don't care how much I weigh. I threw away all my slips from the weighing scales. Going to the gym has been good for me, both mentally and physically, and it has given me confidence in my life.

I love lifting weights and running on the treadmill. When I lift weights, I feel powerful and strong, which makes me feel confident. Sometimes I can't believe how far I have come…it's so humbling. I never gave up, even though at times I was in agony; I kept on moving through the tears and pain.

I still have pelvic girdle pain sometimes, and I suffer from pyriformis syndrome, and sometimes I have sciatica pains. I have learned to listen to my body over the years. I rest when I need to, and workout when I need to. If I have a setback, I might have to walk on the treadmill (which is boring), and then I build myself up again by walking uphill, jogging for a minute, and then, after a few weeks, adding sprinting to my routine.

I generally follow the 80/20 rule when eating. I juice for breakfast, reduce my gluten intake, and don't drink fizzy drinks. I add flax seeds, turmeric, spirulina, nuts, wheatgrass, cinnamon, chia seeds, good fats, and anything that I feel is good for my body, to my food.

I hope that I have shown my children that they should never give up...

Khateeba Chechi

Wow, such strength from these ladies! I really do thank them for their honesty, and I hope it encourages some of you to take action with your own health, before you get a serious wake up call. I know that some ladies have felt they have been selfish in putting themselves first and taking time out to improve their own health, fitness, and confidence, but I think they have been incredibly strong and fantastic role models to their children. They have acknowledged their situation and have been proactive and improved their health, no doubt improving their family's health along the way, and ensuring their children have their mum around for much longer!

My own story was not so dramatic. I had a slipped disc in my upper and lower back, and I finally had to seek medical help from Dr. Gareth when I could no longer do my job. With his help and the expertise of a personal trainer, I was able to realign my spine and strengthen my core, thus improving my overall health and gaining confidence along the way. Dr. Gareth also states that by aligning the spine, you can correct many health issues, including anxiety, digestion problems, and eyesight!

It is very difficult to stay positive and healthy whilst in pain, so it is vital to seek help from an expert to reduce, if not cure, any pain you are in. I am a strong believer in natural cures through manipulation, exercise, and healthy eating, with drugs being a last resort. I am extremely grateful to the many experts whose advice has gotten me to the confident, healthy place I am at today.

ACTION

- What changes can you commit to with your eating habits?
- What games / exercise can you add on a daily or weekly basis?

Food for Thought

Notes

Notes

Chapter 7

It's Magic!

Bring All Your Joy Faster

One of the things that has helped me to live a happier, more confident life is the law of attraction. I haven't put this as a step, as some people may not be able to get their head around it, and I don't want you to think it is only possible to get confidence by using the law of attraction—it's just so much quicker with it!! I was introduced to the LOA many years ago when I was a broke, single mum of two, working in a salon, swamped with stress and bad situations!

I was generally an upbeat person in front of my clients; after all, they come to unload their own problems, not hear mine. But on one occasion, I was particularly down and could not hide it from my client (thank goodness), and on that day, my life took a valuable turn. My first client that day was a lovely lady called Nimi. She listened to my problems, and said, "You need to read this book." She told me of Rhonda Byrnes, and the book, *The Secret*, and briefly explained the law of attraction to me. On that particular day, I was upset about being single and alone, and Nimi said it could help bring a good man into my life. That was enough for me; I was sold! I looked up the book and ended up reading the first two books in the series. Don't bother with the first one; go straight to book two, *The Power*—it is life changing!

The Motivated Mummies' Guide to Confidence

> *"All our dreams can come true
> if we have the courage to pursue them."*
> – Walt Disney

They say you can take a horse to water, but you can't make it drink. Coaching is like that; you can offer to support and help a client, but if the client does not take the action and move their own life forward, you cannot force them. I am telling you that this book is legendary. Many great people have based their careers on it, so look it up and invest the £6; it's a quick easy read that could turn your whole life around.

As I read the book, I had many "aha" moments, and many penny-dropping and dawning realisations. It basically said that I had messed my own life up. Great, a punch in the belly while I'm down, or was it? If I had created this life—this miserable, skint, depressed, single, almost homeless life—then I could create an amazing one too! There are lots of explanation marks in this chapter because I get very excited talking about the LOA! I was in control of my own destiny; I could, through my thoughts and feelings, turn my life around. Ooh, it sounded so exciting. I started straight away, asking the Universe to bring back the man who had just dumped me! Further investigation into LOA clarified that you cannot will someone else to do something; you can only ask for situations that belong purely to you. I started asking the Universe to bring me my perfect man, and if that happened to be the one that just dumped me, then great; if not, the next one would be even better (and he was).

It took a little while to get my perfect man, but I'm talking months, not years. I had some shuffling to do in my life first. The law of attraction encourages you to act *"as if."* So far, I had been acting as a single lady and a single mum of two. I needed to adjust not only my thinking but also some of my physical actions too. Luckily, I had a great bond with my children, and they either trusted me or humoured me, but either way, they went along. Together, we pulled the kitchen table away from the wall so that we could fit a fourth chair around the family table. I cleared out a space in my wardrobe, ready for my perfect man's clothes, and my eldest daughter sat in the back of the car as we travelled, leaving space for my new man.

To some, I must have seemed crazy, but having read up on the law of attraction, and having read many stories of its success, I felt there was absolutely no harm in going ahead and trying. It did not hurt anybody to imagine the best for our lives, although it did take some getting used to. I had always been a half-empty kind of girl. This was my protection mechanism—if you don't get your hopes up, you can't be hurt. But how was that working out for me so far? I hadn't got my hopes up, and I had been hurt many times, so it was time for a new attitude and a new approach.

Tony Robbins often says that if you want different results, you have to take different actions. I use this quote often in my life, in many different situations now. I was trying hard to think positive, and to daydream of the magic that could be: the perfect man that was coming into our lives, and a comfortable and secure future, full of happiness and harmony, after so many years of turmoil and strain.

I didn't stop at just asking for a perfect man. Oh no, once I knew this secret, I decided to use it for every part of my life. I created a vision board of pictures of how I wanted my life to look, and I stuck it on the fridge so I could look at it every day. It included having my own business, a beautiful 4-bedroom home, happy children, a new car, and spare money. Considering, at the time of creating my vision board, I was living in a mortgaged 2-bedroom flat, with the bailiffs after me, close to being homeless, having exhausted all my savings, was single and working for somebody else in their business, life was pretty hard. To go from where I was to where I wanted to be, could have been unimaginable; in fact, before reading *The Secret*, it was unimaginable. I felt there would be no end to the struggles I was facing, and no end to my loneliness; and as a single mum, I was always going to have to fight and work very hard for anything we needed. The law of attraction, above all else, gave me hope. It gave me faith and hope that there could be a better future for me and my children. I have never been a religious person, but I believe that we all need something to hold onto, especially in times of difficulty, and for me, this was a belief I could really get behind. It has given me more courage and strength than I can ever explain.

It took me 1 year to turn my life around. I don't know if that sounds like a long time to you, or a very short time, but considering the mess I was in, it felt like a miracle. I was 32 at the time, but by my 33rd birthday, I had found the man of my dreams. Considering I had been on numerous dating websites, and for years had been on the lookout, I cannot believe that he was literally at the end of my road, just waiting for me to be in the right place at the right time! I do truly believe that we don't always know what is best for us, but the Universe does; and if you are able to let go and just ask the Universe to bring the best for you, that's when magic really does happen. As I said in my wedding speech a few months back, when I met Steve, and he touched me for the first time, I literally felt the sparks between us. It was like chemistry—so strong—and the Universe had literally moved everything to enable us to come together. I'm not a soppy person, but I knew from the very beginning that we were meant to be together, and I find it still quite magical that I manifested Steve into my life.

Not only did I have my perfect man, who came with a dog that my daughters had asked for, I had also manifested my business before meeting him. I was now the proud owner of Tammy's Beauty, which I ran from my living room, and in my eyes, it was a professional salon. I started off doing manicures over an ironing board with a cover draped over it, but I was soon able to manifest my professional manicure table. Having not looked at my vision board for quite a while, I laugh to see that it was exactly the same as the picture on my board—coincidence maybe, but I didn't think so.

It's Magic!

My children's dad was a mechanic, and he kept me in second-hand cars so I could get the children to school. I'm not into cars, so I would struggle to tell you one from another, but I did have a picture of a silver car on my vision board. One day, I got a phone call from their dad, saying that he had a car for me, as mine was almost broken. I got very excited and looked at my vision board to remind myself of the kind of car I would like, and then I went off down to the yard to see what he had. There he was, waiting for me, with a big blue Skoda. I was not disappointed; I was still very grateful to have a car to get from A to B, and even more grateful that I hadn't had to pay for it myself. Gratitude is very important with the law of attraction—if you are not grateful for what you have, you do not get more, and you can even lose what you do have.

So, I was grateful, and I took my new car home and continued on with my week, but it wasn't long before he was calling me again and telling me to come back to the yard. I did, and when I got there, my jaw hit the floor. He had a different car for me that he wanted to swap my Skoda for, and I could not believe it when in front of me was a shiny silver car, exactly like the one on my vision board! Another coincidence? I don't think so! It still gives me goose bumps to think of the things that I have managed to manifest in my life: my own business, my new car, my perfect man, my happy children— and a year after meeting Steve, we moved into a four-bedroom house, which I also manifested! It was way out of our price range, but I would picture us all living there, and I would even drive to it with Heidi, and say, "Let's go home." I had complete and utter faith that it would be our home. I did not know how; I just knew it would.

> *"You do not have to know how it's going to happen.*
> *You just have to know it's going to happen."*
> – Bob Proctor

I do feel truly blessed, and I am very grateful for all the hard times I went through, because they have taught me determination, resilience, and so much more. So, whether you decide to read the book, watch the film, or do your own research into the law of attraction, my advice to you would be: Let go, be grateful for what you have, ask for what you'd like, and trust that the Universe has your back!

*"Logic will get you from A to B.
Imagination will take you everywhere."*
— Albert Einstein

Let's discuss how this law of attraction can be applied when it comes to your confidence. As we have previously discussed, you must take action steps to increase your confidence and build yourself up from where you are now. These steps can be placed on your vision board, along with some powerful pictures of yourself feeling confident, and the words, CONFIDENT, EMPOWERED, BRAVE, DETERMINED, or anything else that feels good to you. For example, if you stated earlier that you were lacking confidence within your family dynamics, you could find a picture of your family, and stick it onto your vision board, with some positive words next to it. Every time you look at the picture, you should feel the feelings that you would like to feel as a happy family. If you had a specific issue—let's say you lack confidence whilst speaking to your mother-in-law—you may stick up a picture of you and your mother-in-law, or just something that symbolises that (a picture of somebody roughly your age, with an older lady), and you could draw a heart around it, and next to it, you could find some words out of a magazine, or write them yourself, such as confident, communicator, kind, caring, etc. You might find pictures of people sitting around a table laughing, or anything that symbolises what you would like to see in your future, and you could stick them onto your vision board.

"Everything you can imagine is real."
— Pablo Picasso

It's Magic!

If you need to gain confidence, and you feel you need to be more authoritative at work, you might find some pictures in a magazine of a lady dressed like a boss, with a briefcase or a laptop. You might find a picture of people in a meeting at work, with a lady standing at the front of the room. These are all symbols that will help you to visualise yourself being confident at work. I suffered with social phobia for almost 20 years, and on my vision board, at the moment, I have pictures of someone at Toastmasters (which is a public speaking group), and I have pictures of people on the phone, because I used to find it very difficult to speak on the phone. I also have a picture of a pile of books, to symbolise my book being published, and if you're reading this, then I guess it came true!

Adapt your vision board with pictures and words of anything and everything that you'd like to see in your future. Nothing is impossible, so let your imagination run wild and your creative juices flow! Fill that vision board with energy and happiness. This is a fantastic activity to do with your children. Teaching them that they can have anything they dream of will be the best start that you could ever give them. My daughter used the secret when she was 11, to get into the local grammar school. She used the techniques I had taught her, and she kept the school prospectus on her desk where she could see it often. She told me that she just imagined that it was already her school. When she looked at the pictures on the front of the cover, she felt happy, as though she had passed her 11+ already, and that she had got accepted into her chosen school. Only three children passed the eleven plus from her school and got into their chosen grammar school. I feel very proud that I was able to teach Heidi this technique and life skill, and she is currently using it as she goes through her GCSE exams. Of course, children need to work hard and put the effort in to achieve, but there is only so much revision a child can do, and having a good attitude toward it, at the same time, works wonders!

*"Exposure from a young age
to the realities of the world is a super-big thing."*
– Bill Gates

Visualisation

Visualisation is a great tool to use to help with confidence, but it's also good in any situation that you find yourself in. They say that if you can think it, you can bring it, and this attitude is extremely common with any of the top athletes these days. If you ask any Olympic competitor what they do before their race, game, or match, they will all tell you the same thing: They visualise themselves winning. There was a study done on athletes some time back, where they wired machines up to the athletes' brains and body muscles and asked them to visualise running their race. It was found that in each person, as they visualised, it fired up the muscles that they would actually be using when participating! So, by visualising, you can actually train the muscles without even using them. Muscles have memory, and when you do an activity over and over again, it becomes easier, because your body remembers the actions. By visualising and firing up those muscles, you are training your body to be ready to take action, and you are much more likely to achieve your goal, as your body has rehearsed it so many times before.

This can work in all different situations. For example, if you are sitting in a waiting room for an interview, you could use your time in two ways: You could sit and wait, and worry about the interview and talk yourself out of it, letting your fears take over; or you could be more proactive, and visualise how you would like the interview to go. This visualising technique helps you to feel more confident, because it's a practice run; but it also works along with the law of attraction. What you think about, you bring about, so by imagining a positive interview, and imagining yourself with lots of confidence, you are more likely to bring that into reality.

It's Magic!

*"Whether you think you can or whether
you think you can't, you're right."
– Henry Ford*

There is a very famous quote by Henry Ford, which you should learn and repeat often, as he sums up both visualisation and the law of attraction. He states in his quote that whatever you believe will happen, will happen. If you believe you can do something, you will do it. You will find a way, and you will continue to keep trying until you achieve it; but if you believe you can't do something, you won't do it. You'll give up, because you believe that you can't do it, so you'll stop trying—it makes complete sense. This is a great quote to pass on to your children. Can you imagine what their life could be like, if they learnt from a young age that if they believed they could do something, then it would happen. Can you imagine their confidence as they succeeded over and over again, because they believed that they could, so they never gave up?

Sometimes we don't allow our children to struggle. I know I have been guilty of this myself, many times. Maybe we have been through painful situations ourselves, and we don't want our children to go through those, so we step in and intervene. We call it caring, and we call it being a good mum, but now I call it selfish. Think back over all the times that you have struggled in life, and all the challenges that you have faced, which you have overcome. Each time you overcame a challenge, you grew, you learnt, and you got stronger. What happens to your child if each time they get a challenge, you fix it for them? How are they ever going to learn to grow and to get stronger? You are robbing your child of their successes.

We do this through love. We love our children so much that we never want to see them hurt, and we never want to see them struggle or be in pain, but we are growing up in a society where our children are being called *snowflakes*, because they cannot handle any situation. They are weak and unprepared. Whose fault is that, if we're being completely honest with ourselves? It's ours. As their mother, we have to take responsibility for how we have raised our children, and just because we have done it out of love does not make it right to continue. Like I say, I am just as at fault as anybody else. When I was at school, I used to hate PE, and sports day was just a nightmare. In my day, we were made to run around the field in front of all the boys, in the ugliest, big green knickers, with our t-shirt tucked in. I was not the slimmest of girls, and my big fat thighs would glow as I got redder and redder, running around the pitch. I hated sports day with a passion. In my eyes, it was just a day to humiliate the non-sporty kids.

When I was in junior school, every year we had a race called the Mini Marathon, where we would all have to run around a track that went around the whole school, including the fields. That was 30 years ago now, and I still remember it like it was yesterday. I remember running past all the parents lined up along the edges, and I use the word, *running*, very loosely—plodding was more accurate. That feeling of being watched at my most embarrassing time—being watched as I felt humiliated because I couldn't keep up with the rest of the children—has stayed with me all these years. I was not massively overweight; I was just quite unfit, and maybe the anxiety that I was feeling didn't help, as it could well have shut down my non-vital organs and made running even harder.

My only saving grace was a heavily overweight kid running behind me. I often wonder how he felt, as just by being overweight carried a large stigma, let alone proving it to everyone by coming last. In my head, I thanked him for being there, because at least I wasn't last! Now I understand why it was done: It's tradition; competition is good; it makes you push yourself harder... or does it? For some, it does. Some people love it; it drives them to be more ambitious, to be better than they were yesterday, and to be better than the next person. But not everybody has that competitive streak, and not everybody feels the need to be better than the other person. Personally, I'm very competitive with myself; I like to push myself harder than I pushed the day before, and I like to be better than I was yesterday. For me, being in that competitive *watched* and *judged* situation only fills me with stress and anxiety, and for me, personally, I do not perform well in those conditions.

I carried this trauma of sports day with me into my adult life, the humiliation clinging to me as tight as those hideous green knickers I had to wear. And when it came to my children having sports day, I tried to save them the pain that I had been through, because I didn't want them to be hurt like I had been hurt, and I didn't want them to carry the trauma with them into their adult lives. Out of love and compassion, I always gave them the option of attending school on sports day. Did I do the right thing? Who knows? I'm only a mum, and I do my best the only way I know how. I could have saved my children from a traumatic event of coming last, but you know what? My children were quite fit and healthy, and not overweight. They probably would never have come last; they could have even come first, so was I saving them from trauma, or was I denying them success? We will never know, because I was too busy controlling the situation and not allowing them to live their lives freely.

I have learnt a huge amount, over the last few years, about why people take the action that they do, and what drives them through life. I made a conscious decision, through my coaching studies, that I would apply every single thing I learnt to my own life first, before asking my clients to apply it to theirs. I wanted to be a good role model and to be an example of what I could help people to achieve, and I thought the best way to do that was to show them my best self, and how much I had changed for the better from my studies. I now allow my children to live as freely as I know how. I am open enough to accept that I can learn more, and I can continue to be a better mum to my children as I continue to grow and learn, but for now, all I can do is give them the best of me, which is a hell of a lot better than it ever was!

*"Learn from yesterday, live for today, hope for tomorrow.
The important thing is not to stop questioning."*
– Albert Einstein

Keeping the Faith

At the moment, my eldest daughter is 19, and she has her own car and a busy life, so she is quite often not home. People always say to me, "I bet you don't sleep until you hear her coming in the door." This is so common for any parents. I often hear stories of shattered mums, as they have waited up until 3am in the morning for their son or daughter to come home from clubbing, or mums with grown up children that cannot settle until they hear that they have arrived home safely after visiting them. I do not have this problem. If Olivia is out, I can easily go to sleep at any time. Is that because I don't love her, and I don't care what she's up to, or if she's safe? Of course not! My girls are my world, but I have learnt self-preservation. I use the law of attraction to keep my children safe, and to keep my own sanity.

As I told you earlier, I used to have panic attacks at the thought of my children dying because I crashed the car; and when they would go away with their dad, I would have palpitations regularly, scared that they would not come back to me because they had died without me there to protect them. This is no way to live. Worrying about your children does not keep them safe. Just because you are sitting up waiting for them does not mean they are going to walk through that door. All it means is that you will be very tired, with big bags under your eyes, the next day. By using the law of attraction, you can have certainty and faith that your child will be home safe and sound when you wake up the next morning.

Now, I'm only human, so I obviously have times when I worry, but when those times pop up, I use visualisation. I visualise my children's future, I see them older with their own children and their busy happy lives, and I focus all my energy and effort on their future happiness.

It's Magic!

What you think about, you bring about, and I believe too strongly in the law of attraction to even think anything negative will happen to my children. I believe, if I am on the frequency of worry and loss in regard to my children, my reality will be worry and loss. If I am on the frequency of happiness, fulfilment, and joy as I visualise their future, my reality will be happiness, fulfilment, and joy, and I will bring more of that into my life.

This concept has not only given me peace of mind, but it has also given my children their freedom to grow, to live, to experience, and to learn. I cannot undo what I have done, but I can move forward in a more positive way, and allow them to reach their full potential in their own unique journey.

"You must expect great things of yourself before you can do them."
– Michael Jordan

ACTION

What easy steps can you take to immerse yourself in the law of attraction?

Get the knowledge
Read books on the law of attraction, frequency, or positive thinking. If you swap 20 minutes of social media scrolling for reading, your life will automatically improve. You will be feeding your brain with powerful information, and changing the way that the neurons in your brain are wired. There is scientific evidence that positive thinking helps you to be more creative and better at problem solving.

Brainwash yourself with clips/YouTube
You have already been brainwashed with society's thoughts, beliefs, and values. It's time now to decide what your own beliefs are, and to brainwash yourself with those. This need not take any extra time; I know you are busy. YouTube and podcasts are great for brainwashing,

and can be played alongside any daily activity. I often listen to a clip while I am getting dressed and doing my hair and makeup (It may only be ten minutes, but you might just hear something that changes your thinking for the whole day.). I also play clips while I am cooking or driving (Chill, I don't watch them; I just listen— it's the same as a radio.), and while I'm eating lunch. This is all *dead* time, which would be wasted with Facebook or watching TV, or just being on autopilot, thinking of nothing in particular. Use this time wisely.

Affirmations
If you have favourite quotes, write them on sticky notes, and post them around your house. Positive affirmations are vital for generating positive self-talk, which promotes confidence and an all-round happier life. There are also free apps you can download that take seconds to read throughout the day, which helps keep you on your good vibe.

Have fun
The law of attraction works on frequency. If you are on a good frequency, good things will happen to you. Positivity breeds positivity. A great example of this is watching people laugh: You have a compulsion to smile, or if they are belly roaring, you just cannot help but laugh too. The mere thought of people having a rip-roaring belly laugh, with tears rolling down their face, and legs crossed trying not to pee, is enough to make anyone let out a little giggle.

One of my favourite suggestions with my mum clients is pillow fighting. I used to do it with my girls when they were young. This is especially good for breaking negative patterns. If you have children that have been arguing or complaining they are bored, grab some cushions or pillows, and give them a good whack! This breaks the cycle because it changes their focus. It also gives them your full attention (It is impossible to text and pillow fight.), it releases energy, and it's a fun activity and a great way for keeping fit. It's a win all round. Please know that this is a friendly whack; I do not condone violence in any way, shape, or form.

Be grateful
Gratitude is the queen of attracting more into your life. What you are grateful for, you will receive more of. Some people keep gratitude journals, but if you are short of time, you can literally just be grateful in your head. A good habit to get into is saying that you're grateful, every morning. This starts your day off in a more pleasant way, and will help you to see the day through rose tinted glasses. Ensure that you feel the feelings of being grateful, as this is the part that super charges all good things for you!

Your past has happened, but your future is in your hands. Your story is not yet written. Make your life count, and be the person you want your child to be.

Notes

About the Author

Tammy is a life coach, speaker, and trainer. She runs regular workshops around the country for her specially picked Motivated Mummies. If you would like to know more about these workshops, or if you would like to work with Tammy to achieve your desired outcome, you can contact her, via her website, at www.motivatedmummies.com.